CHANGING CALIFORNIA TAX RESIDENCY

A Tax Brief

Robert L. Sommers

Sommers-Taxapedia.com

First Edition

ISBN: 978-0-9778616-3-7

Cover art and layout by Crawshaw Design

Sommers-Taxapedia.com

Printed in the United States of America

About the Author

Robert L. Sommers provides sophisticated legal advice concerning complex tax, business and estate planning issues.

As an acknowledged expert in the field of tax law, Bob has written hundreds of articles, columns, and action guides and spoken at dozens of events.

Bob Sommers is The Tax Prophet. He has created and written The Tax Prophet website, a vital resource to those seeking solid U.S. tax information, issue spotting and analysis.

As a full-time practicing attorney in the heart of San Francisco's Financial District, Bob owns and operates a general tax law firm.

He focuses on U.S. and foreign individuals and small companies in the areas of

- Estate planning (wills, trusts and family-based entities)
- Foreign tax
- Business start-ups and funding
- Employee stock options
- Probate and trust administration
- Federal and California tax controversies (audits, appeals and litigation)

Certified as a Tax Specialist by the California Board of Legal Specialization of the State Bar of California (a distinction earned by less than .05% of all attorneys licensed to practice law in California,) Bob also received a postgraduate legal degree (LL.M.) in taxation from New York University School of Law in 1985, the premier graduate tax program in the U.S.

Bob has testified before the US Senate's Finance Committee regarding tax scams on the Internet. He is in demand as an expert witness in both criminal and civil cases involving Tax and Trust Law, Tax Fraud, Busted Tax Shelters, and Bogus Trust Arrangements.

The Wall Street Journal, New York Times, Forbes, CNN to Money magazine and the Best of the Web have all reviewed Bob's work and his contributions to legal education. Reviews online.

CONTENTS

CHANGING CALIFORNIA TAX RESIDENCY

A. Introduction

California is a notorious high-tax state that aggressively pursues its residents who move to another state and contend they no longer owe California taxes. The main bone of contention usually involves stock or security sales, where taxpayers argue they were living in another state (usually a no-tax state) when the asset was sold, with California asserting that the sale occurred while the person was resident in the state and taxes are owed.

B. How High Are the Stakes?

One of the more annoying aspects of California law is there is no capital gains exclusion or reduction, so taxes are calculated at the same rate as ordinary income, which can be as high as 13.3% for incomes exceeding $1,000,000. For example, Elon Musk, the richest person in the world (at the time of this writing), pronounced, quite publicly, that he moved from California to Texas, bragging he sold so much Tesla stock that he paid $12 billion in federal taxes. Since Texas does not have an income tax, he paid no state taxes. Musk purportedly sold stock generating $28 billion in gains.[1] If he is considered a California resident when the stock was sold, he could owe $3.724 billion in California taxes!

---

1 Source: CNBC article "Elon Musk faces a $15 billion tax bill, which is likely the real reason he's selling stock." Update: Musk has since lost $200 billion of his fortune as of January, 2023.

CHANGING CALIFORNIA TAX RESIDENCY

But Musk declared he was a Texas resident so what's the issue? No so fast..... California determines residency by a taxpayer's actions, not their proclamations. According to an interview, Musk made the following statements to TED's Chris Anderson:

> "I don't even own a place right now. I'm literally staying at friends' places," he was quoted as saying by the New York Post.
>
> "If I travel to the Bay Area, which is where most of Tesla's engineering is, I basically rotate through friends' spare bedrooms," the Tesla CEO added.

Guess what? If you had a domicile in California, you must establish a new domicile in another state; otherwise, you remain a California taxpayer and staying at friends' places does not establish a new domicile. Uh-oh, Musk has just shafted himself and admitted he is still a California resident. Intrigued, read on. Musk contends his residence is a rental from his Space-X company, a shack worth $50,000; however, he owned numerous mansions in California, so he'll have a hard time convincing California's Franchise Tax Board (FTB) that the Texas shack he rented constitutes a new domicile.[2] To make matters worse, if the FTB determines that Musk remained a California resident, that determination is presumed correct

2 Note: Staying in California with friends for work at Tesla means he is physically present and engaged in business in California, which rebuts any presumption of non-residency based on the time spent in California, as discussed later in this book.

and Musk must prove that the FTB was wrong in its determination, so it is the taxpayer's burden to prove the FTB is incorrect, which is often difficult, but not insurmountable.

I. CALIFORNIA RESIDENCY RULES

A. Domicile

"Domicile" refers to the place where individuals have their true, fixed, permanent home and principal establishment, and to which place they have, whenever they are absent, the intention of returning.

> "It is the place in which a [person] has voluntarily fixed the habitation of [themselves] and [their] family, not for a mere special or limited purpose, but with the present intention of making a permanent home." (Cal. Code Regs., Title 18, §17014, subd. (c))

To change one's domicile, one must actually move to a new residence and intend to remain there permanently or indefinitely. In re Marriage of Leff (1972) 25 Cal. App. 3d 630, 642. A person may have only one domicile at a time. (Cal. Code Regs., Title 18, § 17014, subd. (c).) One's acts must give clear proof of a current intention to abandon the old domicile and establish a new one. Chapman v. Superior Court (1958) 162 Cal. App. 2d 421.

A domicile cannot be lost until a new one is acquired. Estate of Phillips (1969) 269 Cal.App.2d 656, 659. Once acquired, a domicile is presumed to continue until it is

CHANGING CALIFORNIA TAX RESIDENCY

shown to have changed. 18 Cal. Code Regs. § 17014(c).

Presence within California for more than nine months of a taxable year creates a rebuttable presumption of California residence. Cal. Rev. &Tax. Code § 17016; 18 Cal. Code Regs. § 17016. However, presence within California for less than nine months does not create a presumption of nonresidency. Appeal of Warren L. and Marlys C. Christianson, Cal. St. Bd. of Equal., 72-SBE-022 (July 31, 1972).

However, a person whose domicile is in another state or country will be taxed in California if he or she is found to be a "resident" of California. Similarly, a person who is domiciled in California may escape California tax if he or she is not a "resident" of California. Whether a taxpayer's purpose in entering or leaving California is temporary or transitory in character is essentially a question of fact to be determined by examining all the circumstances of each particular case. Appeal of Michael T. and Patricia C. Gabrik, 86-SBE-014, Feb. 4, 1986.

In our example, Elon Musk has not established that he changed his residence, since he did not move to a new residence, let alone, intended to stay there permanently or indefinitely, since he was frequently returning to California for work.

CHANGING CALIFORNIA TAX RESIDENCY

B. Physical Presence

From Musk's comments, it is unclear how many days a year he spends in California, but if that amount exceeds 6 months during the calendar year, he will be considered a California resident regardless of whether he established a domicile in another state.

California Code of Regulations, Title 18, Section 17014 (b) provides that an individual whose presence in California does not exceed an aggregate of six months within the taxable year, and who is domiciled without the state and maintains a permanent abode at the place of his domicile, will be considered as being in this state for temporary or transitory purposes as long as he does not engage in any activity or conduct in the state other than that of a seasonal visitor, tourist or guest. As noted, Musk continued to work in California which means this statute would not apply.

C. Two Key California Cases

There are two prominent California cases involving taxpayers claiming residency outside of California: Appeal of Bragg, 2003-SBE-002 (2003) and Appeal of Berner, 2001-SBE-006-A (2002).

In Appeal of Bragg, taxpayer's spouse and children lived in California and the children attended school in California. Even so, the Appeals Board ruled that taxpayer spent a majority of

CHANGING CALIFORNIA TAX RESIDENCY

his time in Arizona and only returned to California for visits. Taxpayer's exclusive full-time employment was located in Arizona. Thus, because he lived and worked in Arizona and did not return to California to live with his family, he became a resident of Arizona. The court noted:

> When a California domiciliary leaves the state for purposes of employment, the relevant inquiry is not the type of employment pursued, but whether or not his absence from California is for a temporary or transitory purpose. (citation omitted.) California Code of Regulations, title 18, section 17014, subdivision (b), suggests that when a Californian is employed outside California his absence will be considered for other than a temporary or transitory purpose if the position is expected to <u>last a long, permanent, or indefinite period of time.</u> (citation omitted) [Emphasis added]

In Appeal of Berner, taxpayers were California residents with multiple properties located in the state. Taxpayers contended they moved to Nevada and lived in their California home for approximately four months a year. Taxpayers supplied affidavits from close friends regarding their residency in Nevada, including golf games in Nevada, telephone calls to taxpayers in Nevada and mail delivery and pick-up in Nevada. The Appeals Board ruled that taxpayers were domiciled in Nevada, despite owning a home in California and living there 4 months during the year, noting:

> Consistent with this regulation, the Board has held that the contacts which taxpayers maintain in this and

> other states are important objective indications of whether their presence in, or absence from, California was for a temporary or transitory purpose. (Appeal of Richards L. and Kathleen K. Hardman, 75-SBE-052, Aug. 19, 1975; Appeal of Anthony V. and Beverly Zupanovich, 76-SBE-002, Jan. 6, 1976.)
>
> Such contacts are important as a measure of the benefits and protection that the taxpayers have received from the laws and government of California and as objective indicia of whether the taxpayers entered or left this state for temporary or transitory purposes. (Appeal of Anthony V. and Beverly Zupanovich, supra.)
>
> Thus, if it is determined that appellants [taxpayers] were Nevada domiciliaries, it must also be determined whether their presence in California was <u>for a temporary or transitory purpose.</u> And, if it is determined that appellants were California domiciliaries, it must also be determined whether their presence in Nevada <u>was for a temporary or transitory purpose.</u> [Emphasis added]

Thus, if you want to establish residency outside of California, it is key to establish your domicile and residency in another state, and then make sure you do not return to California except for temporary or transitory proposes. Of course, it is preferable not to come back to California at all, or at least during the 12-month period after you have left the state. If you do return to California, is it best if the trip is for a short vacation or to attend a wedding or family event. Coming back for business purposes will raise issues with FTB as to whether you really left

CHANGING CALIFORNIA TAX RESIDENCY

California in the first place. Note: a corollary argument is if FTB argues you are still domiciled in California, but you actually moved to another state in connection with long-term employment, FTB will have a difficult time establishing that your move was only for temporary or transitory purposes. The lesson here is: it is critical to establish domicile outside of California and not to return here except for short vacations or family-related purposes.

In summary, moving to a residence in another state on a permanent or indefinite basis in connection with long-term full-time employment in that state, then visiting California for non-business purposes and for less than 6 months per year, is sufficient to establish that Taxpayer was not a California resident. To play it safe, wait at least one year before you rely on the 6-month rule, as argued above, stay out of California for the first 12 months of your departure, except for short, family-related purposes. Although there is no rule on this, try not to return to California for more than seven days at a time and only return once or twice during that 12-month period. Finally, note that even if you are a resident of another state, if you are earning income from California sources, that income will be taxed by California, regardless of your residence. This is discussed in detail later in this book.

D. List of Factors to be Considered

The following are a list of factors that the California Board of Appeals considered in Appeal of Bragg. The Board noted that not all factors are weighed equally, but the list "informs taxpayers of the type and nature of connections the respondent (FTB) and this Board find informative when determining residency."

- The location of all of the taxpayer's residential real property, and the approximate sizes and values of each of the residences;
- The state wherein the taxpayer's spouse and children reside;
- The state wherein the taxpayer's children attend school;
- The state wherein the taxpayer takes the homeowner's property tax exemption on a residence;
- The taxpayer's telephone records (i.e., the origination point of taxpayer's telephone calls);
- The number of days the taxpayer spends in California versus the number of days the taxpayer spends in other states, and the general purpose of such days (i.e., vacation, business, etc.);
- The location where the taxpayer files his tax returns, both federal and state, and the state of

residence claimed by the taxpayer on such returns;

- The location of the taxpayer's bank and savings accounts;
- The origination point of the taxpayer's checking account transactions and credit card transactions;
- The state wherein the taxpayer maintains memberships in social, religious, and professional organizations;
- The state wherein the taxpayer registers her automobiles;
- The state wherein the taxpayer maintains a driver's license;
- The state wherein the taxpayer maintains voter registration, and the taxpayer's voting participation history;
- The state wherein the taxpayer obtains professional services, such as doctors, dentists, accountants, and attorneys;
- The state wherein the taxpayer is employed;
- The state wherein the taxpayer maintains or owns business interests;
- The state wherein the taxpayer holds a professional license or licenses;

- The state wherein the taxpayer owns investment real property; and
- The indications in affidavits from various individuals discussing the taxpayer's residency.

E. Selling Your Business or Millions in Stock – Here is Not How to Do It!

If you are going to generate a large capital gain from the sale of your company or other financial assets, such as stock, and you live in California, you can bet FTB will contend you were a California resident on the day of sale. The Bracamonte family learned this lesson the hard way, when their half-baked attempt to claim Nevada residency months before the sale of their janitorial company was rejected by the FTB and California's Office of Tax Appeals in Appeal of J. Bracamonte and J. Bracamonte, OTA Case No. 18010932 (decided March 22, 2021).

The sale occurred on July 18, 2008 (note: it took more than 10 years after the tax return was filed to decide the matter), however, taxpayers moved to Nevada on February 26, 2008 where they rented an apartment, 4.5 months before the sale. The court focused on taxpayers' residency as of the date of sale and concluded they were still domiciled in California. The FTB conceded that taxpayers changed their domicile to Nevada in September, 2008, when they purchased a house, but by then it was too late to alter the taxation of their gains. Regarding the domicile issue, the Court concluded:

> It is uncontroverted that appellants had a California domicile prior to 2008. Despite their purported intent to change their California domicile, appellants did not "adopt some other permanent home" when they took possession of their rented apartment in Henderson, Nevada. Rather, their possession of their apartment was marked with impermanence. Appellants rented the apartment in Henderson, Nevada on March 6, 2008, because, as appellant-husband testified at the oral hearing, they "needed a temporary place to live."
>
> Appellants testified that, as they looked for a permanent home, they decided to secure an apartment in the area of their desired future home to make purchasing a home easier.
>
> Appellants eventually purchased a home in September 2008, but until then, appellants retained their large California home, and left much of their personal property at their California home and spent a majority of their time there from February 25, 2008, through July 18, 2008.
>
> Appellants testified that they only took essentials to their Nevada apartment, such as linens, towels, dishes and some basic furniture. Notably, they left their precious mementos and other valuable items in California until they acquired a "permanent home" in Nevada.
>
> "In order to change one's domicile, one must actually move to a new residence and intend to remain there permanently or indefinitely." (Appeal of Berner (2001-SBE-006-A) 2002 WL 1884256.) Appellants' possession of a rental apartment was part of their plan to find a permanent home, but was not the actual move to a new residence with the intent to remain there permanently.

CHANGING CALIFORNIA TAX RESIDENCY

> The impermanence of the apartment evidences their intention of returning to their California home until they found a suitable Nevada replacement. Consequently, we find that appellants retained their California domicile through July 18, 2008, and did not change their "permanent home" when they took possession of their apartment.

Just look at the number of mistakes taxpayers made in their feeble attempt to change their state tax residency:

1 Taxpayers leased a temporary rental apartment in Nevada: Per the Court's decision, "appellants did not "adopt some other permanent home" when they took possession of their rented apartment in Henderson, Nevada. Rather, their possession of their apartment was marked with impermanence. Appellants rented the apartment in Henderson, Nevada on March 6, 2008, because, as appellant-husband testified at the oral hearing, they "needed a temporary place to live."

Comment: *This is a fatal admission. If you are going to change your residence – do it! Do not engage in a half-baked effort to make the move. If you need to rent, make it at least an annual rental in an unfurnished apartment and move your furniture and belongings from California to the newly rental apartment. Use a moving van and keep the receipts showing that you, indeed, moved all your belongings, pets and valuables to the new location.*

2 "Appellants testified that, as they looked for a permanent home, they decided to secure an apartment in the area of their desired future home to make purchasing a home easier. Appellants eventually purchased a home in September 2008, but until then, appellants retained their large California home, and left much of their personal property at their California home......"

CHANGING CALIFORNIA TAX RESIDENCY

Comment: *You must move your personal property and possessions to your new residence! This is a clear indication that taxpayers did not change domiciles; you need to completely and totally abandon the California domicile in favor of the new one. Do not rent an apartment, then leave your most precious belongings in your California residence. Sell your California residence or rent it out. If you continue to live in it or have it available for future use, you're asking for trouble.*

3 "...and spent a majority of their time there from February 25, 2008, through July 18, 2008. Appellants testified that they only took essentials to their Nevada apartment, such as linens, towels, dishes and some basic furniture. Notably, they left their precious mementos and other valuable items in California until they acquired a "permanent home" in Nevada."

Comment: *No wonder taxpayers lost. They violated the principles set forth in this book – you absolutely cannot spend more time in California than your new place of residence and expect to prevail if the FTB challenges you. Physical presence is probably the strongest indicator in these matters and you need to stay out of California and take your most valuable possessions with you. As the next point illustrates, the court will focus on physical presence – where you are actually living, rather than on your statements of subjective intent. Stated differently, just saying "I intended Nevada to be my permanent residence," while continuing to live in, or frequently visit, California, will not cut it.*

Regarding taxpayers' physical presence, check this out:

4 Most significantly, appellants' physical presence in California from February 26, 2008, the date appellants argue they moved out of California, to July 18, 2008, far outweighed their presence in any other state. As stated above, appellants were in California

for 90 days, and in Henderson, Nevada for only 28 days. We find the sheer amount of time spent in California, and the average length of their stay in the respective homes significant.[3] Indeed, physical presence is a factor of greater significance than mental intent and the formalities that tie one to a particular state. (Noble v. Franchise Tax Bd., supra, 118 Cal.App.4th at pp. 567; Whittell v. Franchise Tax Bd. (1964) 231 Cal.App.2d 278.) Thus, despite appellants' actions to transition to becoming Nevada residents, we find their physical presence in California most persuasive.

Comment: *This reiterates the importance of physical presence and why you need to leave California and not come back. Taxpayers should have lost this case based on the physical presence factor alone. If you learn just one thing from this book, make it this: physical* ***presence is critical*** *to the determination of whether you truly changed your California residence; once you decided to leave California, get out and stay out!*

5 This move is so dumb that I doubt taxpayers had any guidance regarding their conduct:

"Appellants had numerous vehicles and vessels registered in California, including a Harley-Davidson that was purchased in June 2008 and registered in California.

Comment: *I hope everyone can spot this one. Really, you say you changed domicile to Nevada in February, 2008, yet you buy a motorcycle in June, 2008 and register it in California? As propounded repeatedly, you need to get your vehicles out of California and register them in your new place of residence, as well as change your driver's license as soon as possible.*

3 Note: taxpayers averaged 8.5 days per stay in California and just 2.18 days in Nevada, more than 4X the length of stay was in California.

CHANGING CALIFORNIA TAX RESIDENCY

In addition to the foregoing, taxpayers continued to conduct business in California, including the sale of their business and on-going litigation and the Court found that taxpayer's continued physical presence in California after allegedly moving to Nevada far outweighed their presence in any other state and was the most persuasive factor in its analysis.

The lessons here confirm the issues pointed out in this book:

1 Take the residency change seriously, it is a major sacrifice. Don't play games; move your valuable possessions, pets, cars, professionals, and terminate your relationships with California clubs and organizations.

2 Most importantly, for heaven's sake, stay there! Do not come back to California during the year in which the sale occurs and make sure you are out of the state well (preferably 9-12 months) before the tax event. If you cannot do this, then don't bother claiming you've moved from California, because you haven't.

3 If you come back to California, make it for non-business reasons and only stay a couple of days. Plan ahead. If you are going to have a major tax event and are a California resident, move out of California in the year prior to the event and stay out of California during the year the event occurs, except for a couple of short, non-business trips.

4 Start looking for a house in your new state immediately. Contact a realtor and start the house-hunting process right away. It is best to have purchased a house in your new state of residence before you move there (or right after you move there), move everything you own to the

new house and live there as your permanent residence.

5 If possible, accept a job in the state of your new residency prior to moving there or shortly thereafter. This helps explain why you moved to the new state for reasons other than to avoid California tax, although your motivation should not matter because taxpayers are free to lower their taxes by moving to another state.

II. NON-RESIDENTS WORKING IN CALIFORNIA

A. California's Jock Tax - Introduction

The 2015 Super Bowl was played in Levis Stadium. Did you enjoy the Super Bowl? Cheer for your favorite team? California's Tax Man was also clapping for an entirely different reason: the state made a cool $1.0 million in income taxes off the players, because that Super Bowl was played in Santa Clara, California. California earned several millions more from the broadcasters, entertainers and media that gathered for the event. How is this possible? Welcome to California's Jock Tax.

California earned about $239 million (in 2014 – assume that amount has at least doubled in 2022) from taxing athletes on professional teams when they are physically present in California during their sports season. Take Peyton Manning for example: because the Super Bowl was played in California, his tax bill roughly doubled, from $60,000 to $130,000, whether or not he won the

Super Bowl! California does not just tax him on his Super Bowl earnings, he is taxed on a proportionate share of his entire $20 million salary!

B. Apportionment Formula

California taxes the number of "duty days" an athlete spends in California during the entire season, defined as the first official preseason activity to the last game played. Here is the California's Jock Tax regulation (Section 18662-6 (f)(1):

> A "duty day" is defined as "any day services are performed under the contract from the beginning of an official preseason activity until the last game played". The "duty days" in California are then divided by the total "duty days" to create a ratio. This ratio is then multiplied by the total compensation. This then is deemed to be the California source income.

For Payton Manning, the total duty days was 208 (rounded to 200 to illustrate the tax). Manning was in California three days to play the Oakland Raiders and another three days to play the San Diego Charges, or six duty days in total. 6/200 = 3% X his $20 million salary = $600,000 of taxable income to California. Assuming an effective tax rate of 10%, his California tax is $60,000.

The Super Bowl, however, caused him to spend seven days additional in California, thereby increasing his duty days to 13, resulting in an apportionment formula of

13/200 = 6.5% x $20 million = $1.3 million x 10% tax = $130,000, more than his entire Super Bowl winnings. Note, under the formula, his $102,000 of winnings raises his California tax an additional $6,653, because the winnings are added to his salary portion of the calculation.

C. Manning Visits the Tax Prophet

Manning hears about his California tax bill and makes an appointment with yours truly (aka the Tax Prophet). He says, "This can't be right, Tax Prophet lower my taxes!" I notice the vagueness of the terms "duty days" and "official preseason activities" and decide to challenge all implicit assumptions in the formula.

The regulations do not mention how to count duty days when an athlete is in more than one state during the day. Eliminate days in which the team was in California, but the athlete was not, due to injury or other reason (this does not apply to Manning's situation). And what happens when duty days extend to a subsequent calendar year? I conclude that:

- Manning was not in California three days when he played the Raiders and Chargers, he was in Denver for most of the first day. Therefore, remove the first day for both regular season games and the first day of Super Bowl under the same theory, thereby reducing the number of

California duty days from 13 to 10.

- The total number of duty days can be extended if Manning were required to train in Denver as part of his contract. The training sessions must be mandatory and not voluntary. Assume he trained an additional 60 days in Denver as mandated in his contract, thereby increasing the total duty days to 260. His apportionment formula becomes 10/260 = 3.86% and his California taxes drop about 40% to $77,200.

- But let's not stop there. Manning plans on retiring after the Super Bowl so he will not be paid a salary in 2016. So even if he had seven Super Bowl duty days, they occurred in 2016 not 2015, when he earned his $20 million salary. Manning has solid argument that he owes California nothing in 2016 and the apportionment formula contains only the four days he played in California in 2015. Reducing the total duty days by the days in 2016 (37), the formula for 2015 would be 4/233 or 1.72% x $20,000,000 salary = $343,350 x 10% = $34,335, a reduction of $95,665 over the initial calculation of $130,000. Manning, elated with Tax Prophet's wizardry, spikes the ball!

The Lesson: Ambiguity creates opportunity. Challenging the basic assumptions, especially then the terms used are vague, can yield huge tax savings.

CHANGING CALIFORNIA TAX RESIDENCY

D. Why Do Famous Athletes Live in Florida?

I ask Manning why he is resides in Colorado, where he pays income taxes of 4.63%. I explain that his $12 million in endorsement income is fully taxable in Colorado since he lives there, costing him $555,000.

If Manning moved to a non-tax state such as Florida,[4] he'd be $550,000 richer. That's why Derek Jeter, Tiger Woods, Serena and Venus Williams and a host of other professional athletes live in Florida; their endorsement income is shielded from state income taxes.

A more recent example involves NFL star receiver Tyrek Hill and his decision to sign with the Miami Dolphins, rather than the New York Jets. Why? State income taxes was his answer. According to an article in Blumberg News,[5] Hill received a three-year, $120 million contract. Assuming he is paid $40 million a year, he saved closed to $2.7 million in state income taxes by playing for Miami, since Florida is does not have an income tax. Note: Hill still must pay taxes on the days he plays in states with income taxes. If Hill played for any of the three California-based NFL teams, his state income tax would be close to $4.0 million. The Blumberg article quotes a study that

4 Additionally, Nevada, Texas, Alaska, South Dakota, Wyoming and Washington have no income taxes.

5 "Tyreek Hill Moved to Lower His State Taxes, and He's Not Alone" by Jard Walczak

concludes, for each percentage increase in state income taxes a professional sports team winning percentage declines 0.7 percent, close to a 1 to 1 correlation, implying that star players take into consideration state income tax rates.

Although one can question the veracity of this study, there is definitely a tax incentive for a highly-paid professional athlete to play for a team located in a low-tax or no-tax state. Once athletes get wind of this, they may start asking teams in high-tax states to "gross-up" their salary to cover the additional state tax liability imposed on the player. For example, if a football player is considering playing for the San Francisco 49ers or the Miami Dolphins and the proposed salary is $30,000,000 a year, the player would need an additional $4,602,076 to offset California income taxes ($34,602,076 x 13.3% = $4,602,076 in taxes (note: a gross-up amount of $4,588,500 is additional taxable income paid to the player and there is an additional 13.3% tax on this amount); therefore, $34,602,076 - $4,602,076 = $30,000,000 – the equivalent to the $30,000,000 salary if he played for Miami. Note: The owner's financial experts will figure out the state tax credits available in California compared to Florida, but that may impact the calculation by $300,000 or so. It should be noted that top corporate executives sometimes negotiate for a federal tax gross-up on their salaries, so this is a common concept in the tax arena; however, it is a novel application to athletes.

The Rolling Stones and U-2 use the same concept to avoid income taxes on their non- performance income. Their business operations are located in the Netherlands, where the tax on royalty income is extremely low, Entertainers are subject to tax on income earned where physically perform, but they can divert income from their: (i) music royalties and sales; (ii) clothing and product lines; (iii) endorsements; and (iv) other rock star income and sales, to a low-tax jurisdiction.

In fact, Apple, Google, Facebook and a number of U.S. companies pay little or no tax on their earnings outside the U.S. by using the Netherlands royalty law as part of their international tax strategies (called the "Double-Irish Dutch Sandwich"). The same is approach applies to athletes and their endorsement income: move to a state with no income tax.

III. BUT WHAT ABOUT THE REMOTE WORKER?

A. Introduction

Football and rock superstars pay California taxes when they perform in the state, we get that, but what about the average every-day person who works for a California company, but does not step foot into California. A person is taxed either as a resident under the domicile and residency tests discussed above, or on their "California-source" income. Here, the issue is California-source income as the person involved is neither domiciled nor is resident in California.

B. Services are Sourced Where They Are Actually Performed

According to California's Residency and Sourcing Technical Manual:

> In determining whether compensation is California source income [of a taxpayer who is] a nonresident for the entire year, we tax on a source basis.
>
> Income from sources within this State includes income from compensation for personal services performed within this State. (CCR §17951-2)
>
> The critical factor in determining the source of income from personal services is not the residence of the taxpayer, the place where the contract for services is entered into, or the place of payment. It is the place where the services are actually performed. See the Appeal of Janice Rule, 1976-SBE-099, October 6, 1976; Ingram v. Bowers, 47 F. 2d 925, aff'd. 57 F. 2d 65; Appeal of Charles W. and Mary D. Perelle,1958-SBE-057, December 16, 1958; and Appeal of Robert C. and Marian Thomas,1955-SBE-006, April 20, 1955. (Emphasis Added).

Gee, what could be simple than that: Look to the place where the services are actually performed and if the nonresident performs those services outside of California, case closed, no California-source income. It should not matter whether those personal services are performed by a W-2 employee or a Form 1099 independent contractor or a partner or a partnership, a member of a limited liability company or the sole shareholder of an S corporation. Personal services are just that -- personal services -- and there is nothing implying that the employment status of the worker is remotely relevant.

C. The Blair S. Bindley Case – Standing Settled Law on its Head!

Yet, leave it to FTB to contradict the plain working of its own technical manual and claim that a worker performing personal services through as a sole proprietor (an independent contractor) while living in Arizona has California-source income because his "company" is doing business here! Without any fidelity to the concept of personal services as defined in its own technical services manual, FTB wrongly maintains (in my opinion), that an independent contractor or any non-W-2 worker receiving compensation for personal services from a California company has California-source income.

FTB incredulously argues that the test is not where the actual services are performed, but rather that the worker received a benefit (California income) from California – the worker is considered doing business in California and performing services for a California-based consumer. Huh? So, despite the clear and unequivocable language of California's own law regarding the taxation of personal services, the rules do not apply to a sole proprietor (an independent contractor) or, it appears, to any other worker other than a W-2 employee.

And guess what? In a case directly on this issue, Blair S. Bindley, OTA Case No. 18032402 (May 30, 2019), the California Office of Tax Appeals ruled in favor of the FTB and found that personal services performed by a person as a sole proprietor for a California company, were taxable to the service provider, even though he was not domiciled or resident in California. In the Bindley case, the taxpayer performed all the services while physically present in Arizona and there is undisputed tax law on the subject that, under such circumstances, a sole proprietor (independent contractor) is performing personal services that are subject to employment taxes and the services are sourced according to where those personal services are performed (Arizona). Yet, leave it to FTB not to even address this crucial issue and the Office of Tax Appeals (which has a dubious reputation of being a collection of ex-FTB officials[6]) to go along with the FTB without even raising the central issue staring it in the case.

6 Read the bios of the judges and administrative staff https://ota.ca.gov/judges/ and see for yourself how many judges came from private practice with actual real-world experience representing taxpayers and how many are former California FTB or tax appeal employees with little or no actual experience representing taxpayers. I personally know of a situation where a highly-qualified tax attorney in private practice and not a captive of the California tax bureaucracy was rejected for a judgeship. Instead, take a look at the people serving as judges and try to find someone not associated with California's tax bureaucracy.

CHANGING CALIFORNIA TAX RESIDENCY

I wish life were that simple, but it is not. California did pass a law stating those "doing business" in California are taxed on their California-source income, and, evidently, this is supposed to include the situation where the recipient of the services is based in California. See Revenue andTaxation Code Regulation 25136-1. This regulation can be read to contradict R&T Code Section 17951, which is still in full force and effect and has not been amended or deleted from California's tax code, or the new regulation can be read as consistent with Section 17951 in which case, the regulation applies when a person is affirmatively doing business in California, meaning some action, such as performing services in California or having some part of the business operation in California. Nevertheless, any attempt to tax a non-resident on personal service income runs afoul of Section 17951.

Wait, the Court of Appeals did not actually rule that personal services were taxable, they didn't even bother to address the issue! The taxpayer, who had a CPA represent him (not an experienced appellate attorney)[7] apparently didn't even make the argument that personal services performed outside California are not taxable; instead,

7 This is an outrage: CPAs are not trained attorneys, especially appellant-trained attorneys, which is a specialty unto itself. In my opinion, it is the same as having the taxpayer represent themselves which – of course – is an invitation to create bad law that is now legal precedent because FTB, in reality, had no real opposition to its position that directly contradicts Section 17951.

he let the FTB and the Appeals Court run all over him with the argument that the taxpayer was, instead, a company that was doing business in California, so a whole different set of rules would apply.

FTB is aggressively touting their court victory as the proper reading of the situation and many commentators are just repeating FTB's proclamations, without studying the case and understanding the underlying issues. I expect serious future challenges to FTB's position. In the meantime, I have no issue with taking the position that a taxpayer performing personal services outside of California does not have California-source income, because of the express wording of Section 17951, regardless of whether those services are performed as an employee or contractor.

Given the FTB's position and until the California courts clarifies the contradiction between Section 17591 and Regulation 25136-1, one can plan around California's efforts to tax personal services with straight-forward tax planning prior to providing services to a person or company located in California: The non-resident service provider needs to have the service recipient form a corporation outside of California (Nevada, Delaware) and then contract directly with the out-of-state entity. That way, the service provider is performing services for an entity outside of California. All invoices and payments should be between the service provider and the entity with the services or product delivered to the entity. The entity can then pass along the services or products to its California company.

IV. USING A TRUST TO AVOID CALIFORNIA TAXES ON ASSET GAINS

Does a taxpayer really have to move out of California and change their residency to avoid California taxes on the sale of stock or other intangible assets? The answer: with extremely careful planning, a trust can avoid California taxes. For this to work, the trustees need to be non-California residents, the California beneficiary or beneficiaries must have a "contingent" interest in the trust, and the trust needs to be a non-grantor trust (an irrevocable trust). In addition, if the assets are already highly appreciated, there will be federal gift tax issues when funding the trust. So, using a trust makes sense if the assets have not appreciated – such as pre-IPO stock in which the current value is a fraction of the expected future value.

How does such a trust work? A recent California Court of Appeals case, Steuer v FTB, Case A154691 (6/29/2020), provides a roadmap to create a trust that will not be taxed in California, despite having one or more California beneficiaries. In Steuer, the settlor (father) created a trust for his children in which he gave his trustees, one of whom was California resident, complete discretion as to distributions of income and principal to the beneficiaries. The court noted that California-source income would be taxable to the trust, regardless of residencies of the trustee or beneficiaries. If the trust had a California trustee (a situation that should be avoided to make this work), then the trust's income would be apportioned in accordance with the number of California trustees as compared to the total number of trustees. Since in Steuer there were two trustees, one of whom was resident in California, 50% of the non-California source income would be apportioned to California.

Finally, if there were non-contingent beneficiaries residing in California, then some of the income would be apportioned to California, whether or not there were one or more California resident trustees. The court held that since the trustees had "sole and absolute discretion" to make distributions of income and/or principal to the beneficiaries, the beneficiaries were contingent and therefore, not subject to California taxation. This is the critical piece for tax-planning to avoid California taxation.[8] Also, the trust should not have any California trustees to avoid apportionment of income based on the trustee's residence as discussed above.

8 California taxes a resident beneficiary only when that beneficiary's trust interest is not contingent. Cal. Rev. & Tax. Code Ann. §17742 (a).

V. TRUST PLANNING WITH SECTION 1202 STOCK

This planning is especially beneficial to owners of Section 1202 stock (stock in a start-up that must meet certain conditions), since at the time of this writing, the sale of Section 1202 stock is not taxed federally, although California taxes the full amount as ordinary income, subject to a maximum tax rate of 13.3%. In general, Section 1202 stock permits tax-free gains on the sale of $10 million of stock held for at least five years, provided:

- the corporation must be a C corporation and not have more than $50 million in assets when the stock is issued and immediately thereafter;
- 80% of its assets must be in the active conduct of a qualified trade of business (professionals, consultants, athletes, performing arts, financial services, farming and real estate companies are generally excluded from Section 1202 benefits. See IRC Sec 1202(e) for details [9]

Note: Because the stock is transferable by gift under IRC Sec 1202(h), and the benefits accrue to the gift recipient; using one or more trusts to maximize the benefit is not only permitted, it is used as a successful tax-planning strategy by many wealthy investors.

Thus, instead of incurring a California income tax at 13.3%,

9 The Cooley law firm has a flow-chart explaining the ins and outs of Section 1202 – it is attached hereto.

the trust will pay no federal or state income taxes on the sale of Section 1202 stock. For this to work, the stock transfer to the trust should occur when the stock has a low value, since the transaction is subject to gift taxes.

This trust planning is available with respect to other assets located outside of California, such as a securities portfolio or life insurance, but not with California real estate since it is sourced as California property because of its physical location.

VI. CONCLUSION – AVOIDING CALIFORNIA TAX RESIDENCY

From my experience in litigating the California residency issue with FTB, here are my observations and recommendations to avoid California taxes:

1) FTB is going to look at every conceivable source of documentation, all checkbooks and bank accounts, credit cards, and vehicle registration records. In one case, there were several banker's boxes of information FTB required. Also, be prepared to have a diary of each day spent inside and outside California. Unfortunately, the auditor and even the first level of appeals were not very receptive or responsive to taxpayer's evidence and argument, it was only when we met with the actual appeals officer that the case was resolved.

2) Start looking for a residence in another state even before you leave California. Contract a realtor and let them know

CHANGING CALIFORNIA TAX RESIDENCY

you are "permanently" moving and need to purchase a residence. It is critical that you start the process of house-hunting as soon as possible, preferably with a signed contract with a realtor. In contrast, FTB will not believe you permanently moved out of California if you rent a furnished apartment.

3) In fact, state you are leaving California permanently whenever you communicate about your move, in your emails, resignation letters, and social media posts.

4) Although California case law says FTB cannot took at gym or club memberships as a factor, it does anyway, so it is best to write letters/emails resigning from gym or club memberships, stating that you are permanently moving to another state. In one case I handled, the taxpayer resigned from her long-time book club, stating she was permanently moving to another state and FTB treated this as evidence of her intent to change residence.

5) Hire a moving company to move your belongings. FTB zeroed in on the fact that my client did not hire a moving van (her relative had a van and moved her belongings) we needed to overcome this fact with sworn statements that the relative did, in fact, move the taxpayer's belongings. If you hire a moving van (of course, retain the receipt!) you can use this as positive evidence that you intended to permanently move from California.

CHANGING CALIFORNIA TAX RESIDENCY

6) To the extent your move is job-related, having a letter from your employer stating that they need you to live and work in the state you are moving to on a permanent basis will provide additional evidence that your move from California is not temporary or transitory.

7) If you are selling stock or other intangible investment asset, FTB will look at the time leading up to your sale and will try to claim that you were still a California resident before you sold the asset. However, FTB will also look at your actions after you sold the asset to determine whether your actions were consistent with changing your residence outside of California. So do not move to another state, sell your asset and then move back to California, at least for several years after you sold the asset. There is no hard and fast rule, but waiting a minimum of three years (five years is better), is a good rule of thumb.

LIST OF EXHIBITS

Exhibit "A" Appeal of Bragg, 2003-SBE-002 (2003)

Exhibit "B" Appeal of Berner, 2001- SBE-006-A (2002)

Exhibit "C" FTB Publication 1031 – Guidelines for Determining Resident Status

Exhibit "D" Appeal of J. Bracamonte and J. Bracamonte, OTA Case No. 18010932 (decided March 22, 2021)

Exhibit "E" Blair S. Bindley, OTA Case No. 18032402 (May 30, 2019)

Exhibit "F" Steuer v FTB Court of Appeals, Case A154691 (6/29/2020)

Exhibit "G" Cooley – Section 1202 Qualified Small Business Stock Checklist

Exhibit "A"

2003-SBE-002

BEFORE THE STATE BOARD OF EQUALIZATION

OF THE STATE OF CALIFORNIA

In the Matter of the Appeals of	)	
	)	
Stephen D. Bragg	)	Nos. 110567 and 119357
	)	

Representing the Parties:

For Appellant:	Jon H. Lieberg, Esq.
For Respondent:	Charlene L. Woodward, Tax Counsel III
Counsel for Board of Equalization:	Reed Schreiter, Tax Counsel

O P I N I O N

These appeals are made pursuant to section 19045[1] of the Revenue and Taxation Code from the action of the Franchise Tax Board on the protests of Stephen D. Bragg[2] against proposed assessment of additional personal income tax in the following amounts: $48,153 for the year 1993; and, $42,658 and a late filing penalty in the amount of $10,664 for the year 1995. The appeals present two issues for our consideration: 1) Whether appellant was a resident of

[1] Unless otherwise specified, all section references are to sections of the Revenue and Taxation Code as in effect for the years in issue.

[2] Appellant and his former wife, Cecilia M. Bragg, filed a 1993 joint tax return. On April 7, 1994, however, appellant filed for a divorce from Cecilia Bragg; the divorce became final on July 25, 1995. Cecilia Bragg filed a separate appeal, and thus the term "appellant" as used herein refers only to Stephen D. Bragg.

This appeal is made pursuant to section 19045 of the Revenue and Taxation Code[1] from the action of the Franchise Tax Board on the protest of Raymond H. and Margaret R. Berner against a proposed assessment of additional personal income tax in the following amounts: $95,691.00 tax and a notice and demand penalty of $23,922.75 for 1986; $313,694.00 tax and a notice and demand penalty of $78,423.50 for 1987; and, $49,672.00 tax and a negligence penalty of $3,932.90 for 1988. The primary issue here is whether appellants were residents of California for tax years 1986 through 1988. Respondent argues that this Board's previous decision for tax year 1985 (in which we concluded that appellants were California domiciliaries and residents) is binding on our consideration of the present years. Appellants argue that our 1985 decision was not final because the parties entered into a settlement agreement concerning 1985 (approved by the trial court, but agreed by the parties to not affect subsequent tax years).

Facts and Contentions

Appellants were long-term domiciliaries and residents of California prior to their marriage in 1980. At that time they moved into a 4,637 square foot home in Solana Beach, California (San Diego County) which appellant-husband had purchased in 1977. In December 1980, they purchased a 1,550 square foot home in Stateline, Nevada. Also in 1980, appellant-husband inherited his mother's 1,808 square foot San Diego condominium. These were the three residences owned through 1985 that were the basis of this Board's prior decision—for years 1981 through 1985. For those prior years, the Board concluded that appellants had failed to carry their burden of proof that their domicile had changed from California to Nevada. The present appeal raises the same issues of residency and domicile that were before the Board for 1981 through 1985. However, since the Board's prior decision found that appellants had not established a change in domicile for 1981 through 1985, the further issue raised is whether the Board's prior decision binds it in any way for the present years.

Respondent argues that the Board's prior decision—that appellants were domiciliaries and residents of California for 1985—is the necessary starting point for the present appeal. It argues that the issue of domicile for 1985 was previously litigated and decided by the Board—therefore, the doctrine of collateral estoppel forbids the issue to be relitigated for years 1981 through 1985. Respondent argues, in effect, that this Board must base the present opinion upon the fact that appellants were domiciliaries of California on December 31, 1985. This would require appellants to carry the burden of proving that their domicile changed from California to Nevada on or after January 1, 1986—

[1] Unless otherwise specified, all section references are to sections of the Revenue and Taxation Code in effect for the years in issue.

he and his wife adopted two children. The children attended California schools, with the exception of approximately three months in 1993 when one child attended school in Arizona while living with appellant.

From 1965 until 1988, appellant worked in a family-owned crane company headquartered in Long Beach, California. Appellant apparently managed the company's operations outside California, which required appellant to be outside California on a regular basis. Appellant concedes he continued to be domiciled in California during this period, and his time outside California was for a temporary or transitory purpose only. In 1988, appellant sold his interest in the family crane company in order to devote himself to fulfilling his dream of becoming a rancher. Appellant, doing business as Rancho Milagro, apparently began cattle ranching operations in Arizona and California in 1989. Although Rancho Milagro maintained some ranch operations in California, the majority of ranch property and ranch employees were located in Arizona. Appellant owned a large tract of land in Arizona and leased land adjacent thereto for purposes of grazing cattle. Apparently, this approach was more cost effective than purchasing feed due to the modest price of land in Arizona. Land prices in California precluded purchasing large tracts of land for purposes of grazing cattle.

On approximately April 1, 1993, appellant moved to the Arizona ranch property and began the process of counting and branding cattle pursuant to a contract with Farm Credit. Appellant states the contract allowed him 120 days to accept or reject a cattle count on forest service property adjacent to the Arizona property. Initially, appellant apparently slept in a bedroll and lived in a tent. Later, he lived in a double-wide ranch trailer without electricity or a telephone. Appellant managed the ranch operations, which employed approximately 20 people and consumed 70 to 90 hours per week of appellant's time. Appellant's many duties included buying, selling, vaccinating, de-licing, tagging, and gathering cattle. Appellant indicated his duties as ranch owner/manager constituted his exclusive full-time employment.

During 1993, appellant also held interests in the following: An 80-acre cutting horse ranch and a cattle feeding operation in Temecula, California; a 50-percent interest in a subchapter S corporation engaged in cattle trading and feeding in Brawley, California; a cattle hauling business in Brawley; a partnership interest in a Texas horse breeding syndicate; a partnership interest in a California limited partnership engaged in housing development; an interest in a subchapter S corporation operating a vocational school; and cattle trading in California, Arizona, and Mexico.

Beginning in 1985, appellant purchased three parcels of real property located in Temecula, California, on which appellant built a 6,500 square foot custom home and established a commercial cutting horse operation and a cattle feed operation. The residence constituted the family's primary residence. Appellant states he claimed the homeowner's exemption on the residence through 1995. Respondent asserts appellant tried to sell the residence in 1993. Appellant counters that the attempted sale occurred in 1992 and that until he filed for divorce in 1994 he intended to return to the Temecula residence. Appellant's former wife received the Temecula residence and property in the divorce settlement. Appellant also purchased residential real property in Santa Ana, California, in 1991. Appellant's adult daughter received the Santa Ana property in the divorce settlement and now lives in the residence. Appellant purchased a ranch in Texas in 1993, which he deeded to his former wife in the divorce, and a time-share in Puerto Vallarta, Mexico, which appellant and his former wife apparently continued to co-own.

Appellant maintained bank accounts in both California and Arizona. Appellant contends during the period at issue he and his wife utilized the California accounts as their personal accounts, while the Arizona accounts served as business accounts. Appellant asserts his accountant, attorneys, physician, dentist, and chiropractor were located in California.

Appellant states he did not register to vote in Arizona until April 1995, while respondent asserts appellant cancelled his California voter registration on September 24, 1991. Respondent's auditor's notes indicate the registrar of voters for Riverside County, California, advised that appellant transferred his voter registration from Riverside County to "another county," effective September 24, 1991. A registrar of voters in Arizona apparently advised respondent that appellant was "registered to vote since [April 17, 1995]," and that prior to that date appellant was registered to vote in Yavapai County, Arizona.

Appellant and his wife maintained and registered numerous personal and business vehicles in California and Arizona. Appellant states the vehicles registered in Arizona served as business vehicles only. Appellant further indicates he was cited by Arizona authorities for driving a vehicle registered in Arizona with a California driver's license. As a result, appellant states he surrendered his California license and obtained an Arizona driver's license. Respondent contends appellant's California driver's license was suspended on April 10, 1992. Appellant counters that his California license expired on December 27, 1993, and that any suspension was for a violation in California.

Appellant filed his 1993 Arizona tax return in August 1994 and his 1993 California tax return in September 1994. Both returns, signed under penalty of perjury, indicated appellant's address as being in New River, Arizona, and his occupation as rancher. Both returns also stated appellant changed his residence from California to Arizona as of April 1, 1993. Appellant's Arizona and federal tax returns for 1994 and 1995 also indicated appellant's address as New River, Arizona.

Appellant states the parties agree that appellant was a California resident in 1992 and an Arizona resident in 1994. The question thus becomes appellant's residence in 1993.

Appellant appears to contend he was domiciled in California and was outside the state for a temporary or transitory purpose only. Respondent, on the other hand, appears to contend appellant was a domiciliary and resident of Arizona. It is against this background that we consider the rules governing residency status.

California imposes income tax liability upon the entire taxable income of every resident, and upon the entire taxable income derived from sources in California of every nonresident or part-year resident. (Rev. & Tax. Code, § 17041, subds. (a)(1) & (b).) The term "resident" includes individuals in this state for other than a temporary or transitory purpose, and individuals domiciled in this state who are outside the state for a temporary or transitory purpose. (Rev. & Tax. Code, § 17014, subds. (a)(1) & (a)(2).) The primary consideration under either facet of the definition is whether or not the individual is present in California or absent from California for a temporary or transitory purpose. (*Appeal of Anthony V. and Beverly Zupanovich*, 76-SBE-002, Jan. 6, 1976.)

The determination of whether or not an individual is present in or absent from California for a temporary or transitory purpose depends largely upon the facts and circumstances of each case. (Cal. Code Regs., tit. 18, § 17014, subd. (b); *Appeal of Raymond H. and Margaret R. Berner*, 2001-SBE-006-A, Aug. 1, 2002; *Appeal of David A. Abbott*, 86-SBE-104, June 10, 1986.) The determination cannot be based solely on the individual's subjective intent, but must instead be based on objective facts. (*Appeal of Anthony V. and Beverly Zupanovich, supra.*) In situations where an individual has significant contacts with more than one state, the state with which the individual maintains the closest connections during the taxable year is the state of residence. (Cal. Code Regs., tit. 18, § 17014, subd. (b); *Appeal of Raymond H. and Margaret R. Berner, supra.*)

Consistent with this view, the contacts the individual maintains in this and other states are important objective indications of whether the individual's presence in or absence from California was for a temporary or transitory purpose. (*Appeal of David J. and Amanda Broadhurst*, 76-SBE-036, Apr. 5, 1976.) In past decisions, the Board considered connections such as maintenance of a family home, business interests, bank accounts, retention of the services of professionals licensed under state law, membership in religious or social organizations, and ownership of real property. (*Appeal of Anthony V. and Beverly Zupanovich, supra.*) Such connections are important as a measure of the benefits and protections the individual received from the laws and government of California. (*Appeal of David J. and Amanda Broadhurst, supra.*)

The California Court of Appeal and respondent's regulations define "domicile" as the location where a person has the most settled and permanent connection, and the place to which a person intends to return when absent. (*Whittell v. Franchise Tax Board* (1964) 231

Cal.App.2d 278, 284; Cal. Code Regs., tit. 18, § 17014, subd. (c).)[5] An individual may claim only one domicile at a time. (Cal. Code Regs., tit. 18, § 17014, subd. (c).) While an individual's intent will be considered when determining domicile, intent will not be determined merely from unsubstantiated statements; the individual's acts and declarations will also be considered. (*Appeal of Joe and Gloria Morgan,* 85-SBE-078, July 30, 1985.) In order to change domicile, a taxpayer must actually move to a new residence and intend to remain there permanently or indefinitely. (*In re Marriage of Leff* (1972) 25 Cal.App.3d 630, 642; *Estate of Phillips* (1969) 269 Cal.App.2d 656, 659.)

Respondent's determinations of residency are presumptively correct, and the taxpayer bears the burden of showing error in those determinations. (*Appeal of Joe and Gloria Morgan, supra.*) The burden of proof as to a change of domicile is on the party asserting such change. (*Sheehan v. Scott* (1905) 145 Cal. 684, revd. on other grounds in *Zeilanga v. Nelson* (1971) 4 Cal.3d 716; *Appeal of Terance and Brenda Harrison*, 85-SBE-059, June 25, 1985.) If there is a doubt on the question of domicile after presentation of the facts and circumstances, the domicile must be found to have not changed. (*Whitmore v. Commissioner* (1955) 25 T.C. 293; *Appeal of Anthony J. and Ann S. D'Eustachio*, 85-SBE-040, May 8, 1985.)

Although it is difficult to enunciate a specific test for determining residency due to the variety of factual contexts in which the residency question can arise, we will reiterate the purpose of the residency rules, which underlies all our decisions, and identify a list of factors which our experience informs us can be helpful in determining where an individual's closest connections lie, and thus where an individual's presence is for other than a temporary or transitory purpose. We are mindful at this juncture that the factors serve merely as a guide in our determination of residency. Thus, the weight given to any particular factor depends upon the totality of the circumstances. The focus of our examination is to determine where an individual is present for other than a temporary or transitory purpose, not whether or not an individual satisfies a majority, or even a significant number, of the factors.

The purpose of the residency statute is to insure that all individuals who are in California for other than a temporary or transitory purpose enjoying the benefits and protection of the state should in return contribute to its support. (Cal. Code Regs., tit. 18, § 17014, subd. (a); *Whittell v. Franchise Tax Board, supra,* 231 Cal.App.2d at p. 285.) A review of prior decisions of this Board and the California courts reveal an extensive list of objective factors used to determine with which state the taxpayer's closest connections lie. The following list of factors may not be exhaustive, but certainly informs taxpayers of the type and nature of connections respondent and this Board find informative when determining residency:

---

[5] The court of appeal also stated the law may assign a domicile to an individual constructively. (*Whittell v. Franchise Tax Board, supra,* 231 Cal.App.2d at p. 284.)

- The location of all of the taxpayer's residential real property, and the approximate sizes and values of each of the residences;
- The state wherein the taxpayer's spouse and children reside;
- The state wherein the taxpayer's children attend school;
- The state wherein the taxpayer claims the homeowner's property tax exemption on a residence;
- The taxpayer's telephone records (i.e., the origination point of taxpayer's telephone calls);
- The number of days the taxpayer spends in California versus the number of days the taxpayer spends in other states, and the general purpose of such days (i.e., vacation, business, etc.);
- The location where the taxpayer files his tax returns, both federal and state, and the state of residence claimed by the taxpayer on such returns;
- The location of the taxpayer's bank and savings accounts;
- The origination point of the taxpayer's checking account transactions and credit card transactions;
- The state wherein the taxpayer maintains memberships in social, religious, and professional organizations;
- The state wherein the taxpayer registers his automobiles;
- The state wherein the taxpayer maintains a driver's license;
- The state wherein the taxpayer maintains voter registration, and the taxpayer's voting participation history;
- The state wherein the taxpayer obtains professional services, such as doctors, dentists, accountants, and attorneys;
- The state wherein the taxpayer is employed;
- The state wherein the taxpayer maintains or owns business interests;
- The state wherein the taxpayer holds a professional license or licenses;
- The state wherein the taxpayer owns investment real property; and
- The indications in affidavits from various individuals discussing the taxpayer's residency.

During the year at issue, appellant owned a personal residence in Temecula with his wife for which they claimed the homeowner's property tax exemption. Appellant, however, concedes he and his wife attempted to sell this residence in 1992; appellant provided no explanation of where he and his wife intended to live if they had sold the residence. Appellant and his wife owned a second residence in Santa Ana, which later became their daughter's residence, and a time-share in Puerto Vallarta, Mexico. For a greater percentage of the period in question, appellant's wife and children remained in California and the children attended California schools. Appellant, however, spent a majority of his time in Arizona, returning to California for visits.

Appellant and his wife claimed Arizona residency on their state and federal returns filed in 1993, although they later amended the state returns to reflect California residency. The 1993 tax returns indicated an Arizona mailing address. Appellant and his wife maintained a number of bank accounts in both California and Arizona, as well as owning and registering a number of vehicles in both California and Arizona. Appellant claimed the personal (in contrast to the business) accounts and vehicles were located in California. Appellant stated he obtained all his professional services in California. Appellant indicated he owned real property in California, Arizona, and Texas.

Appellant owned business interests in California, Arizona, and Texas. Appellant admitted his exclusive full-time employment consisted of his cattle ranching duties in Arizona. Neither party discusses the nature of appellant's involvement in the other business ventures. Given his 70 to 90 hour work week on the Arizona ranch, however, we anticipate his cattle ranching duties necessarily limited his activities in the other business ventures.

Section 17104, subdivision (a), makes no distinction with respect to employment.[6] When a California domiciliary leaves the state for purposes of employment, the relevant inquiry is not the type of employment pursued, but whether or not his absence from California is for a temporary or transitory purpose. (*Appeal of Joe and Gloria Morgan, supra.*) California Code of Regulations, title 18, section 17014, subdivision (b), suggests that when a Californian is employed outside California his absence will be considered for other than a temporary or transitory purpose if the position is expected to last a long, permanent, or indefinite period of time. (*Appeal of David A. Abbott, supra.*)

Although appellant contends he went to Arizona for a 120-day period in order to brand and count cattle pursuant to a contract with Farm Credit, he also indicated his lifelong desire to be a rancher. The record indicates appellant did not return to live in California at the conclusion of the 120-day period, nor do we find any evidence to suggest appellant intended to return to California, despite the various factors discussed above that might suggest appellant maintained California residency. To the contrary, the record supports a conclusion that appellant began in 1988 to lay the groundwork for his permanent move to the Arizona ranch in 1993. In 1988, appellant sold his interest in the family business; in 1989, he purchased ranch property in Arizona and California, and began ranching operations in which the majority of the land and employees were located in Arizona; in 1990, he attended a ranching-for-profit course in Albuquerque, New Mexico; and, in 1993, appellant moved to the Arizona ranch.

---

[6] Section 17104, subdivision (c), does make certain distinctions for elected and appointed officials and their staffs, which are not relevant in this appeal.

In further support of our conclusion, we note appellant's family lived with him in Arizona for a period of time in 1993, but returned to California in early 1994. Appellant apparently did not make adequate provision for his family to live with him in Arizona. Appellant did not return to California with his family, nor did he subsequently return to California despite owning several residences. In fact, appellant filed for divorce from his wife shortly after her return to California, and he remains in Arizona to this day. Finally, we believe appellant's claim of Arizona residency on his 1993 tax returns merely reflects his residency status as he believed and intended it to be. We thus conclude respondent properly determined appellant was a resident of Arizona in 1993. We believe this conclusion properly reflects the fact that appellant, although a California resident at one time, left the state in 1993 for other than a temporary or transitory purpose.

The second issue presented by these appeals arises from appellant's execution of a purchase and sales agreement in September 1988 for the sale of his one-third interest in Bragg Investment Company, Inc., as well as his interests in several other corporations and family partnerships. The purchase and sales agreement contains a covenant-not-to-compete, which precluded appellant from participating in competing business activities for a period of 10 years in 30 counties in California, 2 counties in Nevada, 35 counties in Oregon, and 39 counties in Washington. The annual covenant payment was $1,333,333.00, and appellant's one-half community property interest was $666,666.50.

The parties disagreed as to the correct apportionment percentage to apply to the income received by appellant attributable to the covenant-not-to-compete. Respondent determined 84.05 percent of the covenant income should be apportioned to California, while appellant concludes 25.00 percent is more appropriate. Appellant appears to base this calculation on the fact that he forfeited his right to conduct business in four states, and thus each state counts equally in determining the apportionment of the income.

The *Appeals of Paul B. and Mary A. Milhous, et al.* (2000-SBE-003), decided November 2, 2000 (*Milhous*), represents our most recent discussion of whether California may tax income from a covenant-not-to-compete executed in connection with the sale of a business. In that appeal, we addressed three issues related to imposing tax on income from a covenant-not-to-compete. The first holding emerging from the case is that the right to compete is a property right with its situs in the location where such competition would have occurred absent the covenant. Second, we determined that the source of income from a covenant-not-to-compete is the place where the promisor promised not to act. Finally, we adopted a three-factor formula used to assign business income attributable to a state as the methodology for determining what portion of the covenant income should be assigned to California. We noted that adopting the standard three-factor apportionment formula used in the Uniform Division of Income for Tax

Purposes Act (UDITPA)[7] allowed for the use of an alternative formula in the event the standard three-factor formula would lead to an unfair representation of the extent of the taxpayer's activities in California. We stated the three-factor formula "rightfully sources covenant income to the places where the promisor forfeited the right to act in amounts that reflect the degree of corporate activity within the prohibited area." (*Appeals of Paul B. and Mary A. Milhous, et al., supra.*)[8]

Appellant contends the income from the covenant-not-to-compete is not California-source income, arguing that the word "source" conveys the idea of origin or the place where the services are actually performed. Appellant then argues respondent's use of the Bragg Investment Company apportionment factors is erroneous. Appellant states the allocation of income to California has no rational relationship to the source of the Bragg Investment Company as payee. Appellant, instead, argues that both actors and athletes use a duty-day formula and advocates this is the proper approach in this case.

Appellant indicates respondent used the alleged apportionment formula for Bragg Investment Company of 84.05 percent to calculate the proper apportionment of his income from the covenant-not-to-compete to California. Appellant contends respondent fails to provide information or documentation as to how it arrived at this percentage. Further, appellant contends the use of the apportionment formula places a burden on a taxpayer to file a return based on information to which the taxpayer may have no access.

Initially, respondent comments on an argument raised by appellant during the protest hearing. Respondent apparently disallowed losses from Tac-Fumasi Ranch, Ltd., and Health Staff Training Institute. Upon review, respondent allowed those losses as California-source losses and computed a revised tax liability for appellant, which is reflected in the figures set forth at the outset of this opinion.

Respondent indicates that appellant annually received $1,333,333 from the covenant-not-to-compete. Respondent states appellant and his wife reported this amount on his 1992 federal and California income tax returns. In 1993, however, when appellant moved to Arizona, respondent indicates appellant and his wife excluded this source of income from their California nonresident tax return. Upon audit, respondent added these sources of income back into appellant's California return and used the Bragg Investment Company 1989 apportionment factor of 84.05 percent to apportion the covenant-not-to-compete income to California.

---

[7] See Rev. & Tax. Code, §§ 25120 – 25139.

[8] The "three-factor" apportionment formula found in UDITPA looks to the taxpayer's property, payroll, and sales in the states in which the taxpayer is carrying on business activities and compares those numbers with the taxpayer's total property, payroll, and sales.

Respondent states it used the Bragg Investment Company apportionment factor for 1989, the year after appellant's sale, since appellant failed to timely report the income and apportionment factor for 1988.

In *Milhous*, we adopted the three-factor formula used to assign business income attributable to a state for purposes of UDITPA as the methodology for determining what portion of the covenant income should be assigned to California. Our review of the record before us indicates that respondent properly applied our precedent from *Milhous*. Appellant fails to convince us that the standard three-factor formula is inappropriate in this case. Further, we find respondent's use of the apportionment factor for 1989 rather than 1988 appropriate, particularly in light of evidence to suggest the 1989 factor was more favorable to appellant and appellant had access to the apportionment information as a major shareholder.

In conclusion, we hold that respondent properly determined appellant to be an Arizona resident in 1993 and that respondent properly included the covenant-not-to-compete income in appellant's California income utilizing the apportionment factor for 1989.

ORDER

Pursuant to the views expressed in the opinion of the Board on file in this proceeding, and good cause appearing therefor,

IT IS HEREBY ORDERED, ADJUDGED, AND DECREED, pursuant to section 19047 of the Revenue and Taxation Code, that the actions of the Franchise Tax Board on the protests of Stephen D. Bragg against proposed assessment of additional personal income tax in the amount of $48,153 for the year 1993, and against proposed assessment of additional personal income tax in the amount of $42,658 and a late filing penalty of $10,664 for the year 1995 are hereby sustained.

Done at Sacramento, California, this 28th day of May 2003, by the State Board of Equalization, with Board Members Ms. Carole Migden, Mr. Claude Parrish, Mr. Bill Leonard, Mr. John Chiang, and Ms. Marcy Jo Mandel present.

Carole Migden, Chairwoman

Claude Parrish, Member

Bill Leonard, Member

John Chiang, Member

*Ms. Marcy Jo Mandel, Member

* For Steve Westly per Government Code section 7.9

Bragg_rs

Exhibit "B"

2001-SBE-006-A

BEFORE THE STATE BOARD OF EQUALIZATION

OF THE STATE OF CALIFORNIA

In the Matter of the Appeal of	)	
	)	No. 88344
Raymond H. and Margaret R. Berner	)	
	)	

Representing the Parties:

For Appellants:	Richard L. Dewberry, Esq. Joseph A. Vinatieri, Esq.
For Respondent:	Natasha Sherwood Page, Tax Counsel
Counsel for Board of Equalization:	Donald L. Fillman, Tax Counsel Craig R. Shaltes, Tax Counsel III

OPINION ON PETITION FOR REHEARING

Background

Upon consideration of the petition for rehearing filed by respondent, we hereby restate and amend our original opinion as indicated below. In its petition, respondent requests the Board to change the wording of our discussion regarding respondent's consideration of declaratory evidence and our discussion about the applicability of the doctrine of collateral estoppel. We believe a change in our original opinion as to the collateral estoppel argument is warranted; in all other aspects, our original opinion remains the same. Therefore, in amending our opinion, we hereby withdraw our previous opinion in this appeal, dated December 20, 2001, and replace it with this opinion; we deny respondent's petition for rehearing, because the arguments set forth in the petition do not constitute sufficient grounds to grant a rehearing. (See *Appeal of Wilson Development, Inc.*, 94-SBE-007, Oct. 5, 1994.)

This appeal is made pursuant to section 19045 of the Revenue and Taxation Code[1] from the action of the Franchise Tax Board on the protest of Raymond H. and Margaret R. Berner against a proposed assessment of additional personal income tax in the following amounts: $95,691.00 tax and a notice and demand penalty of $23,922.75 for 1986; $313,694.00 tax and a notice and demand penalty of $78,423.50 for 1987; and, $49,672.00 tax and a negligence penalty of $3,932.90 for 1988. The primary issue here is whether appellants were residents of California for tax years 1986 through 1988. Respondent argues that this Board's previous decision for tax year 1985 (in which we concluded that appellants were California domiciliaries and residents) is binding on our consideration of the present years. Appellants argue that our 1985 decision was not final because the parties entered into a settlement agreement concerning 1985 (approved by the trial court, but agreed by the parties to not affect subsequent tax years).

Facts and Contentions

Appellants were long-term domiciliaries and residents of California prior to their marriage in 1980. At that time they moved into a 4,637 square foot home in Solana Beach, California (San Diego County) which appellant-husband had purchased in 1977. In December 1980, they purchased a 1,550 square foot home in Stateline, Nevada. Also in 1980, appellant-husband inherited his mother's 1,808 square foot San Diego condominium. These were the three residences owned through 1985 that were the basis of this Board's prior decision—for years 1981 through 1985. For those prior years, the Board concluded that appellants had failed to carry their burden of proof that their domicile had changed from California to Nevada. The present appeal raises the same issues of residency and domicile that were before the Board for 1981 through 1985. However, since the Board's prior decision found that appellants had not established a change in domicile for 1981 through 1985, the further issue raised is whether the Board's prior decision binds it in any way for the present years.

Respondent argues that the Board's prior decision—that appellants were domiciliaries and residents of California for 1985—is the necessary starting point for the present appeal. It argues that the issue of domicile for 1985 was previously litigated and decided by the Board—therefore, the doctrine of collateral estoppel forbids the issue to be relitigated for years 1981 through 1985. Respondent argues, in effect, that this Board must base the present opinion upon the fact that appellants were domiciliaries of California on December 31, 1985. This would require appellants to carry the burden of proving that their domicile changed from California to Nevada on or after January 1, 1986—

[1] Unless otherwise specified, all section references are to sections of the Revenue and Taxation Code in effect for the years in issue.

and the only facts that the Board should consider are those occurring after 1985. For reasons discussed later in this opinion, the Board rejects this premise.

The following transactions occurred during the years presently in issue with respect to appellants' residences: (1) in November 1986, appellants purchased a 2,684 square foot home in Glenbrook, Nevada (near Stateline, Nevada); (2) in September 1988, appellants purchased a 2,773 square foot home in Indian Wells, California; and (3) in November 1988, appellants sold their 4,637 square foot home in Solana Beach, California.

Respondent examined the present three years (1986 through 1988) as a result of its former audit. When no returns were filed, respondent contacted appellants. Appellants then filed a California Nonresident Personal Income Tax Return for 1988 only. This was the year appellants sold the Solana Beach home for $750,000, with resultant California-source income. Respondent issued Notices of Proposed Assessment (NPA) for each year based on appellants' federal returns. From the information it gathered, respondent concluded that appellants had the closest connection, during 1986 through 1988, with California. It further concluded that appellants did not show evidence of a change of domicile from California to Nevada during the three years in issue. Thus, respondent contends that appellants never permanently left California.

Respondent noted that appellants had a membership in a country club near their home in Solana Beach, California, which was used extensively until September 1988, when they purchased their home in Indian Wells, California. Appellants then joined a country club in Indian Wells, California, in November 1988. Respondent contends that appellants' utility bills from California were larger than those from Nevada for all three years. Respondent used cancelled checks that it obtained from the Bank of America in Nevada to conclude that more of the type of contacts that correspond with a residence occurred in California than Nevada for the years in issue. Included were purchases of goods and services, including contacts with medical and dental offices and weekly maintenance of the California home (housekeeper, gardener, pool service, and security). Respondent also attempted to reconstruct the number of days that appellant spent each year in California and Nevada (appellants also traveled to other states and countries during this period). Of the days for which respondent believes it could account, it concluded that appellants spent more days in California than Nevada in 1986 and 1988, and more days in Nevada than California in 1987. Respondent also concluded that appellants made more bank deposits in California than Nevada in each year, and had more credit card transactions in California in 1986 and 1988, but more in Nevada for 1987. Respondent also noted that appellants had retained a California attorney to represent them in the dispute with respondent.

Appellants contend that they spent approximately four months each year in California, seven months in Nevada, and one month elsewhere. They contend that the time spent in California was primarily during the winter months when there was snow at their home in Nevada, although appellants acknowledge that they spent most of the Christmas holidays in Nevada. Appellants dispute respondent's conclusions concerning days spent in California and Nevada, as well as respondent's conclusions from the credit card usage and bank transactions. They indicate that some of the credit card transactions attributed by respondent to California were actually transactions that occurred when they crossed the border near Stateline or when a business near Stateline used a California bank. Appellants provided documentary evidence to support this contention. They also provided evidence that extensive catalog purchases were made while residing in Nevada from California based mail order vendors that respondent contended were California credit card transactions.

Appellants contend that appellant-husband's frequent golf games were much more frequent in Nevada than California—but there were no country clubs to join (during those years) near their Nevada residence. Thus, nearby public courses (without the same record keeping) were the ones used while living in Nevada. With their supplemental brief dated February 9, 2001, appellants provided over 30 affidavits and declarations from friends, relatives, and professional individuals concerning appellants' contacts with Nevada. Golfing friends stated that they had played golf with appellant-husband in Nevada throughout the year, or in California during the period of January through April, or visited appellants in their Nevada home at various times of the year. Several affidavits support appellants' contention that more time was spent in Nevada than in California during the years in issue. Several indicate that the signatory kept in contact with appellants frequently by telephone at the Nevada residence—not the California residence. Several indicate that appellants' lives were centered in Nevada. One affidavit is from the Postmaster of Glenbrook, Nevada, indicating that he had became familiar with appellants when they came to pick up their mail, at least weekly; and, when appellants were on vacation they would provide directions for handling their mail.

Appellants also noted that during the years in issue they: each had a Nevada driver's license; were registered to vote in Nevada; used a Nevada bank; registered most of their automobiles in Nevada; and, maintained their permanent home and abode in Nevada. They contend that their retention of a residence in California, and their use of that residence, was consistent with that of a seasonal visitor to California. Appellants did not claim a homeowners' tax exemption on any of the California property.

Applicable Law

Burden of Proof and Presumptions on Appeal. Respondent's determination of an assessment is presumed correct and appellant has the burden of proving it to be wrong. (*Todd v. McColgan* (1949) 89 Cal.App.2d 509; *Appeal of Myron E. and Alice Z. Gire*, 69-SBE-029, Sept. 10, 1969; *Appeal of Ismael R. Manriquez*, 79-SBE-077, Apr. 10, 1979.[2]) Respondent's determination of residency is also presumptively correct. (*Appeals of John R. Young*, 86-SBE-199, Nov. 19, 1986.) The burden of proof as to a change of domicile is on the party asserting such change.

[2] State Board of Equalization ("SBE") opinions can be viewed on our website (www.boe.ca.gov).

(*Sheehan v. Scott* (1905) 145 Cal. 684, revd. on other grounds in *Zeilanga v. Nelson* (1971) 4 Cal.3d 716; *Appeal of Terance and Brenda Harrison*, 85-SBE-059, June 25, 1985.) If there is doubt on the question of domicile after the facts and circumstances have been presented, the domicile must be found to have not changed. (*Whitmore v. Commissioner* (1955) 25 T.C. 293; *Appeal of Anthony J. and Ann S. D'Eustachio*, 85-SBE-040, May 8, 1985.) Respondent's imposition of most penalties, including those in issue, is also presumed correct (see, e.g., *Appeal of W. L. Bryant*, 83-SBE-180, Aug. 17, 1983; *Appeal of Robert Scott*, 83-SBE-094, Apr. 5, 1983; and *Appeal of Thomas T. Crittenden*, 74-SBE-043, Oct. 7, 1974).

Domicile and Residency. Section 17041 imposes a tax on every "resident" of California. Section 17014, subdivision (a), assigns resident status to "[e]very individual who is in this state for other than a temporary or transitory purpose." Subdivision (b) deals with California domiciliaries who are absent from the state, and provides that every such individual "who is outside the state for a temporary or transitory purpose" is a resident. The key question under either subdivision is whether the taxpayer's purpose in entering or leaving California was temporary or transitory in character. This determination cannot be based on the taxpayer's subjective intent, but must instead be based on objective facts. (*Appeals of Nathan H. and Julia M. Juran*, 68-SBE-004, Jan. 8, 1968.)

Proof of Non-Residence. California Code of Regulations, title 18 (Regulation), section 17014, subdivision (d), states that the type and amount of proof cannot be specified by general regulation. However, ordinarily affidavits or testimony of an individual and of his friends, employer, or business associates that the individual was in California for rest or vacation will be sufficient to overcome any presumption of residency in California. Regulation section 17014, subdivision (b), provides that an individual whose presence in California does not exceed an aggregate of six months within the taxable year, and who is domiciled without the state and maintains a permanent abode at the place of his domicile, will be considered as being in this state for temporary or transitory purposes provided he does not engage in any activity or conduct in the state other than that of a seasonal visitor, tourist or guest.

Whether a taxpayer's purpose in entering or leaving California is temporary or transitory in character is essentially a question of fact to be determined by examining all the circumstances of each particular case. (See *Appeal of Michael T. and Patricia C. Gabrik*, 86-SBE-014, Feb. 4, 1986.) In situations where the taxpayers have significant contacts with more than one state, as appellants do here, the state with the closest connections during the taxable year is the state of residence. (Cal. Code Regs., tit. 18, § 17014, subd. (b).) Consistent with this regulation, the Board has held that the contacts which taxpayers maintain in this and other states are important objective indications of whether their presence in, or absence from, California was for a temporary or transitory purpose. (*Appeal of Richards L. and Kathleen K. Hardman*, 75-SBE-052, Aug. 19, 1975; *Appeal of Anthony V. and Beverly Zupanovich*, 76-SBE-002, Jan. 6, 1976.) Such contacts are important as a measure of the benefits and protection that the taxpayers have received from the laws and government of California and as objective indicia of whether the taxpayers entered or left this state for temporary or transitory purposes. (*Appeal of Anthony V. and Beverly Zupanovich*, *supra*.)

"Domicile" refers to the place where individuals have their true, fixed, permanent home and principal establishment, and to which place they have, whenever they are absent, the intention of returning. "It is the place in which a [person] has voluntarily fixed the habitation of [themselves] and [their] family, not for a mere special or limited purpose, but with the present intention of making a permanent home." (Cal. Code Regs., tit. 18, § 17014, subd. (c).) In order to change one's domicile, one must actually move to a new residence and intend to remain there permanently or indefinitely. (*In re Marriage of Leff* (1972) 25 Cal.App.3d 630, 642.) A person may have only one domicile at a time. (Cal. Code Regs., tit. 18, § 17014, subd. (c).) One's acts must give clear proof of a current intention to abandon the old domicile and establish a new one. (*Chapman v. Superior Court* (1958) 162 Cal.App.2d 421.) However, a person whose domicile is in another state or country will be taxed in California if he or she is found to be a "resident" of California. Similarly, a person who is domiciled in California may escape California tax if he or she is not a "resident" of California.

Thus, if it is determined that appellants were Nevada domiciliaries, it must also be determined whether their presence in California was for a temporary or transitory purpose. And, if it is determined that appellants were California domiciliaries, it must also be determined whether their presence in Nevada was for a temporary or transitory purpose. (See discussion, *supra*, regarding whether a taxpayer's purpose for entering or leaving California is temporary or transitory in character.)

Res Judicata (Including Collateral Estoppel). The doctrine of res judicata gives conclusive effect to a prior judgment or decision. It has two aspects: (1) the prior judgment is a complete bar to a subsequent action so far as the subsequent action is on the same cause of action; and (2) the prior judgment is conclusive as to issues actually litigated between the parties in the former action if the subsequent action is on a different cause of action. Thus, under the second aspect, "collateral estoppel" (issue preclusion)[3] forbids a party from relitigating the same issues even if the cause of action is different. (See 7 Witkin, *supra*, §281, p. 821; *Bernhard v. Bank of America* (1942) 19 Cal.2d 807; *Appeal of Eli A. and Virginia W. Allec*, 75-SBE-004, Jan. 7, 1975.) Collateral estoppel has been applied in tax cases. (*Calhoun v. Franchise Tax Board* (1978) 20 Cal.3d 881.)

The Second Restatement of Judgments, section 13, provides as follows:

---

[3] The term "collateral estoppel" was used in the first Restatement of Judgments, and is now in common use. The Second Restatement of Judgments uses the term "issue preclusion." (7 Witkin, Cal. Procedure (4th ed. 1997) Judgment, §354, p. 915.)

> "However, for purposes of issue preclusion (as distinguished from merger and bar), 'final judgment' includes any prior adjudication of an issue in another action that is determined to be *sufficiently firm* to be accorded conclusive effect."

(Emphasis added.) This concept was applied in *Sandoval v. Superior Court* (1983), 40 Cal.App.3d 932, 937, where the court applied collateral estoppel to a trial court judgment—even though the parties reached a post-decision settlement. The court stated: "the Restatement analysis and reason itself dictate that the trial court judgment reemerges with sufficient finality to permit the application of collateral estoppel." (*Id.*) Thus, we conclude that the Board's decision for the prior years (1981—1985) was a final decision, notwithstanding the fact that the parties reached a subsequent settlement.

However, we note that the doctrine of collateral estoppel is "not an inflexible, universally applicable principle; policy considerations may limit its use where the limitation on relitigation underpinnings of the doctrine are outweighed by other factors." (*Jackson v. City of Sacramento* (1991) 117 Cal.App.3d 596, 603.) In the present appeal, appellants have presented substantially more evidence in support of their position than they did in their previous appeal. Therefore, we choose not to apply collateral estoppel to this appeal.

Penalties. Former section 18683 (renumbered to § 19133, operative Jan. 1, 1994) provides that, if a taxpayer fails to file a return upon notice and demand by respondent, the taxpayer will incur a penalty unless the taxpayer can establish that "the failure is due to reasonable cause and not willful neglect." The penalty is computed as 25 percent of the total tax, determined without regard to payments or other credits. (*Appeal of Robert Scott, supra.*) To establish reasonable cause, a taxpayer must demonstrate that he or she exercised ordinary business care and prudence. (*Appeal of Stephen C. Bieneman*, 82-SBE-148, July 26, 1982.) In order to overcome the presumption of correctness of a penalty, the taxpayer must provide credible and competent evidence to support the claim of reasonable cause; otherwise, the penalty will not be abated. (*Appeal of Winston R. Schwyhart*, 75-SBE-035, Apr. 22, 1975.)

Former section 18684 provided for a "negligence" penalty of five percent of the total amount of the applicable deficiency.[4] Negligence includes any failure to make a reasonable attempt to comply with the provisions of the Internal Revenue Code. In the present appeal, appellants failed to file a timely California Personal Income Tax return for 1988 even though they sold the Solana Beach, California, residence (acquired in 1977) for $750,000. Respondent imposed the penalty for negligence only for tax year 1988. We held in *Appeal of Greg L. Dexter*, decided on May 6, 1986, as follows:

[4] Former section 18684 was repealed effective July 31, 1990. It was replaced by section 19164 (which incorporates the provisions of Internal Revenue Code section 6662) and provides for an "accuracy-related" penalty, including a penalty for negligence, of 20 percent of the applicable underpayment.

> "[A] deficiency is the difference between the taxpayer's correct tax liability and the amount of tax shown on his original return. In the case where a delinquent return is filed, the tax shown on such return does not reduce the amount of the deficiency. [Citations omitted.] Since appellant did not file a timely return, a deficiency existed in the amount of his total tax liability, and the negligence penalty was properly computed on that amount."

Thus, an underpayment is not reduced by the amount of tax liability shown on a return that is not timely filed.

Conclusions

We conclude that appellants have established through affidavits and declarations of friends, family, and professionals (sufficient proof under Regulation section 17014, subdivision (d)) that they changed their domicile from California to Nevada, effective for each of the three tax years in issue, and their primary residence for each of these years was in Nevada. We find from the declarations that appellants' presence in California did not exceed six months in any taxable year and that their activity in this state was that of a seasonal visitor. The fact that the appellants owned a home in California and belonged to a California golf club does not change these findings. The fact that appellants utilized the services of a California attorney should have no effect on the determinations. We also conclude that appellants have established reasonable cause for failing to file California personal income tax returns for the two tax years in which they did not have California-source income (1986 and 1987). Therefore, the proposed tax on non-California-source income is reversed and the notice and demand penalties imposed for 1986 and 1987 will be abated. For 1988 (the year which appellants eventually filed a late return showing California-source income), we conclude that the portion of the negligence penalty applicable to the California-source income was proper; the remaining portion of this penalty will be abated.

We also find that respondent should ordinarily follow the evidence guideline of Regulation section 17014, subdivision (d), which it adopted pursuant to Revenue and Taxation Code (former) section 9253, and current section 19503. In this case, respondent failed to reasonably consider the declarations and evidence provided by appellants.

We deny respondent's petition for rehearing, and restate and amend our original decision as indicated above.

ORDER

Pursuant to the views expressed in the opinion of the Board on file in this proceeding, and good cause appearing therefor,

IT IS HEREBY ORDERED, ADJUDGED, AND DECREED, pursuant to section 19047 of the Revenue and Taxation Code, that the petition for rehearing filed by respondent is denied and that our original opinion in this matter is restated and amended as reflected in the attached written opinion. The action of the Franchise Tax Board on the protest of Raymond H. and Margaret R. Berner against a proposed assessment of additional personal income tax in the amounts of $95,691.00 and penalty of $23,922.75 for 1986, $313,694.00 and penalty of $78,423.50 for 1987, be and the same are hereby reversed. The action of the Franchise Tax Board on the protest against a proposed assessment of additional personal income tax in the amount of $49,672.00 and penalty of $3,932.90 for tax year 1988, be and the same are hereby modified to include only the tax and penalty applicable to California-source income.

Done at Sacramento, California, this 1st day of August, 2002, by the State Board of Equalization, with Board Members Mr. Chiang, Mr. Klehs, Mr. Parrish, and Ms. Marcy Jo Mandel present.

Mr. John Chiang, Chairman

Mr. Johan Klehs, Member

Mr. Claude Parrish, Member

*Ms. Marcy Jo Mandel, Member

____________________, Member

*For Kathleen Connell per Government code section 7.9.

berner_crs

FTB STATE OF CALIFORNIA
Franchise Tax Board

Exhibit "C"

FTB Publication **1031**

2021
Guidelines for Determining Resident Status

Table of Contents

ONLINE SERVICES

Go to **ftb.ca.gov** for:

- **MyFTB** – view payments, balance due, and withholding information.
- **Web Pay** – to pay income taxes. Choose your payment date up to one year in advance.
- **CalFile** – e-file your personal income tax return.
- **Refund Status** – find out when we authorized your refund.
- **Installment Agreement** – request to make monthly payments.
- **Subscription Services** – sign up to receive emails on a variety of tax topics.
- Tax forms and publications.
- FTB legal notices, rulings, and regulations.
- FTB's analysis of pending legislation.
- Internal procedure manuals to learn how we administer law.

2021 Guidelines for Determining Resident Status

A Introduction

It is important for California income tax purposes that you make an accurate determination of your residency status. Residency is primarily a question of fact determined by examining all the circumstances of your particular situation. This publication provides information to help you determine the following:

- Whether you are a resident of California.
- Whether your income is taxable by California.
- Which form to file if you have a California filing requirement.

The Franchise Tax Board (FTB) issues written advice on whether a particular activity or transaction is subject to tax under California income tax law. The FTB will not issue written opinions on whether you are a California resident for a particular period of time because residency is a question of fact, not law. The information included in this publication is provided to help you with this determination.

In general, California nonresidents or part-year residents determine their California tax by multiplying their California taxable income by an effective tax rate. The effective tax rate is the California tax on **all** income as if you were a California resident for the current tax year (and for all prior taxable years for any carryover items, deferred income, suspended losses, or suspended deductions) divided by that income.

This method ensures that nonresidents pay the correct tax on their California sourced income and does not tax non-California sourced income.

For more information, get FTB Pub. 1100, Taxation of Nonresidents and Individuals Who Change Residency.

Registered Domestic Partners (RDP)

Under California law, RDPs must file their California income tax returns using either the married/RDP filing jointly or married/RDP filing separately filing status. RDPs have the same legal benefits, protections, and responsibilities as married couples unless otherwise specified.

If you entered into a same sex legal union in another state, other than a marriage, and that union has been determined to be substantially equivalent to a California registered domestic partnership, you are required to file a California income tax return using either the married/RDP filing jointly or married/RDP filing separately filing status.

For purposes of California income tax, references to a spouse, husband, or wife also refer to a California RDP, unless otherwise specified. When we use the initials RDP they refer to both a California registered domestic "partner" and a California registered domestic "partnership," as applicable. For more information on RDPs, get FTB Pub. 737, Tax Information for Registered Domestic Partners.

Military Personnel and Spouses

In addition to this publication, military personnel and spouses should use FTB Pub. 1032, Tax Information for Military Personnel.

B Basic Filing Requirements

Residents – File a California tax return if either your gross income (which consists of all income you received from all sources in the form of money, goods, property, and services, that is not exempt from tax) or your adjusted gross income (which consists of your federal adjusted gross income from all sources, reduced or increased by all California income adjustments) is more than the amounts shown on the chart below for your filing status, age, and number of dependents.

Nonresidents and Part-Year Residents – File a California tax return if you have any income from California sources and your gross income (which consists of all income you received from all sources in the form of money, goods, property, and services, that is not exempt from tax) or adjusted gross income (which consists of your federal adjusted gross income from all sources, reduced or increased by all California income adjustments) is more than the amounts shown on the chart below for your filing status, age, and number of dependents.

Note: If your gross income or adjusted gross income is less than the amounts listed on the chart, you may still have a filing requirement. For more information, get California Form 540 Personal Income Tax Booklet or California Form 540NR Nonresident or Part-Year Resident Booklet.

On 12/31/21, my filing status was:	**and on 12/31/21, my age was:** (If your 65th birthday is on January 1, 2022, you are considered to be age 65 on December 31, 2021)	**California Gross Income**			**California Adjusted Gross Income**		
		Dependents			**Dependents**		
		0	1	2 or more	0	1	2 or more
Single or head of household (Get FTB Pub. 1540, Tax Information for Head of Household Filing Status)	Under 65 65 or older	19,310 25,760	32,643 35,760	42,643 43,760	15,448 21,898	28,781 31,898	38,781 39,898
Married/RDP filing jointly Married/RDP filing separately (The income of both spouses/RDPs must be combined; both spouses/RDPs may be required to file a tax return even if only one spouse/RDP had income over the amounts listed.)	Under 65 (both spouses/RDPs) 65 or older (one spouse/RDP) 65 or older (both spouses/RDPs)	38,624 45,074 51,524	51,957 55,074 61,524	61,957 63,074 69,524	30,901 37,351 43,801	44,234 47,351 53,801	54,234 55,351 61,801
Qualifying widow(er)	Under 65 65 or older		32,643 35,760	42,643 43,760		28,781 31,898	38,781 39,898
Dependent of another person Any filing status	Any age	More than your standard deduction (Use the California Standard Deduction Worksheet for Dependents, in the instructions for your tax return, to figure your standard deduction.)					

Even if you do not meet the basic filing requirements, you should still file a tax return in order to get a refund if any of the following apply:

- California state income tax was withheld from your pay, California real estate sale, or income from an S corporation, partnership, or Limited Liability Company (LLC).
- You made California estimated tax payments.
- You have withholding from Form(s) 592-B, Resident and Nonresident Withholding Tax Statement, or 593, Real Estate Withholding Statement.

C Which Form to File

Residents – If you were a full-year resident of California in 2021 and you meet the basic filing requirements outlined in Section B, file either Form 540 or 540 2EZ, California Resident Income Tax Return.

However, if you file a joint return and either spouse/RDP was a nonresident or a part-year resident in 2021, file Form 540NR, California Nonresident or Part-Year Resident Income Tax Return.

Nonresidents and Part-Year Residents – If you were a full-year nonresident of California in 2021 and you meet the basic filing requirements outlined in Section B, or if you were a California resident for part of the year, file Form 540NR.

D Filing Status

Use the same filing status for California that you used for your federal income tax return, unless you are an RDP. If you are an RDP and file single for federal, you must file married/RDP filing jointly or married/RDP filing separately for California. If you are an RDP and file head of household for federal purposes, you may file head of household for California purposes only if you meet the requirements to be considered unmarried or considered not in a domestic partnership. If you did not file a federal return because you did not have a federal filing requirement, you may use any filing status on your California return that you were entitled to use on your federal return had you been required to file a federal return.

Exception: If you file a joint return for federal purposes, you may file separately for California if either spouse was one of the following:

- An active member of the United States armed forces or any auxiliary military branch during 2021.
- A nonresident for the entire year and had no income from California sources during 2021.

Regardless of your residency status, if you file separate California returns, enter the amount you would have reported if you had filed a married filing separate return when the instructions for the California return say to enter an amount from your federal return. Attach an explanation to your California return showing how you split the income from your joint federal return between you and your spouse. If you are required to attach a copy of your federal return to your California return, attach a copy of your joint federal return.

For RDP filing status information, get FTB Pub. 737.

E Who Are Residents and Nonresidents

A **resident** is any individual who meets any of the following:

- Present in California for other than a temporary or transitory purpose.
- Domiciled in California, but outside California for a temporary or transitory purpose. See Section L, Meaning of Domicile.

A **nonresident** is any individual who is not a resident.

A **part-year resident** is any individual who is a California resident for part of the year and a nonresident for part of the year.

Safe Harbor

Safe harbor is available for certain individuals leaving California under employment-related contracts. The safe harbor provides that an individual domiciled in California who is outside California under an employment-related contract for an uninterrupted period of at least 546 consecutive days will be considered a nonresident unless any of the following is met:

- The individual has intangible income exceeding $200,000 in any taxable year during which the employment-related contract is in effect.
- The principal purpose of the absence from California is to avoid personal income tax.

The spouse/RDP of the individual covered by this safe harbor rule will also be considered a nonresident while accompanying the individual outside California for at least 546 consecutive days.

Return visits to California that do not exceed a total of 45 days during any taxable year covered by the employment contract are considered temporary.

Individuals not covered by the safe harbor determine their residency status based on facts and circumstances. The determination of residency status cannot be solely based on an individual's occupation, business, or vocation. Instead, consider all activities to determine residency status. For instance, students who are residents of California leaving this state to attend an out-of-state school do not automatically become nonresidents, nor do students who are nonresidents of California coming to this state to attend a California school automatically become residents. In these situations, individuals must determine their residency status based on their facts and circumstances, as described in Section G, Guidelines for Determining Residency, and Section H, Temporary or Transitory Purposes.

Example 1 – You are a California resident. You agreed to work overseas for one year. You returned to California after the employment contract expired and stayed for three months. Then, you signed another contract with the same employer to work overseas for another year. You cannot be considered a nonresident under the safe harbor rule because your absence from California for employment reasons was not for an uninterrupted period of at least 546 consecutive days. You cannot combine the days you were overseas from the two separate contracts.

Example 2 – You are a California resident. You transferred to your employer's Germany office for a two-year work assignment. You visited California for a three-week vacation. Under the safe harbor rule, you were a nonresident of California for the two years you were in Germany. Your three-week visit to California is considered temporary.

Example 3 – You and your spouse are California residents. You agreed to work overseas for 20 months under an employment contract. Your family remained in San Diego, CA. During those 20 months you visited your family in San Diego for a month. You can be considered a nonresident during your absence under the safe-harbor rule. Your month-long visit to California is considered temporary. During the year, you earned $80,000 on your overseas assignment and your spouse earned $30,000 as a teacher in San Diego. You did not have any other income. The tables on the next page show how to report income if you filed a joint income tax return or separate income tax returns.

Joint Return			
Income		Return for You and Your Spouse Form 540NR	
		Total AGI	CA AGI Sch CA (540NR) Col. E
Your Wages	$80,000	$80,000	$40,000*
Spouse's Wages	$30,000	$30,000	$30,000
Total Wages	**$110,000**	**$110,000**	**$70,000**

Separate Returns			
Income	Your Return Form 540NR		Your Spouse's Return Form 540
	Total AGI	CA AGI Sch CA (540NR) Col. E	Total AGI Sch CA (540) no adjustments
Your Wages	$40,000	$0	$40,000*
Spouse's Wages	$15,000	$15,000	$15,000
Total Wages	**$55,000**	**$15,000**	**$55,000**

*Half of your wages are taxable to California because California is a community property state and your spouse/RDP is a resident of California.

F Significance of Residency

Residency is significant because it determines what income is taxed by California. For more information, see Section I, Income Taxable by California.

G Guidelines for Determining Residency

The underlying theory of residency is that you are a resident of the place where you have the closest connections.

The following list shows some of the factors you can use to help determine your residency status. Since your residence is usually the place where you have the closest ties, you should compare your ties to California with your ties elsewhere. In using these factors, it is the strength of your ties, not just the number of ties, that determines your residency. This is only a partial list of the factors to consider. No one factor is determinative. Consider all the facts of your particular situation to determine your residency status.

Factors to consider are as follows:

- Amount of time you spend in California versus amount of time you spend outside California.
- Location of your spouse/RDP and children.
- Location of your principal residence.
- State that issued your driver's license.
- State where your vehicles are registered.
- State where you maintain your professional licenses.
- State where you are registered to vote.
- Location of the banks where you maintain accounts.
- The origination point of your financial transactions.
- Location of your medical professionals and other healthcare providers (doctors, dentists, etc.), accountants, and attorneys.
- Location of your social ties, such as your place of worship, professional associations, or social and country clubs of which you are a member.
- Location of your real property and investments.
- Permanence of your work assignments in California.

Note: If you are impacted by the COVID-19 pandemic, it is one of the factors we will consider as we apply the general rules for residency and income sourcing included in this publication. For more information related to COVID-19 pandemic, go to **ftb.ca.gov** and search for **covid-19**.

H Temporary or Transitory Purposes

Generally, your state of residence is where you have your closest connections. If you leave your state of residence, it is important to determine if your presence in a different location is for a temporary or transitory purpose. You should consider the purpose and length of your stay when determining your residency. Military personnel and spouses, get FTB Pub. 1032.

Coming into California

When you are present in California for temporary or transitory purposes, you are a nonresident of California. For instance, if you come to California for a vacation, or to complete a transaction, or are simply passing through, your purpose is temporary or transitory. As a nonresident, you are taxed only on your income from California sources.

When you are in California for other than a temporary or transitory purpose, you are a California resident. For instance, if your employer assigns you to an office in California for a long or indefinite period, if you retire and come to California with no specific plans to leave, or if you are ill and are in California for an indefinite recuperation period, your stay is other than temporary or transitory. As a resident, you are taxed on income from all sources.

You will be presumed to be a California resident for any taxable year in which you spend more than nine months in this state.

Although you may have connections with another state, if your stay in California is for other than a temporary or transitory purpose, you are a California resident. As a resident, your income from all sources is taxable by California.

Example 1 – You are a business executive and reside in New York with your family. Several times each year you travel to other states for business purposes. Your average stay is one or two weeks and the entire time spent in California for any taxable year does not exceed six weeks. Your family usually remains in New York when you are traveling for business purposes.

Determination: Under these circumstances, you are not a California resident because your stays in California are temporary or transitory in nature. As a nonresident, you are taxed only on your income from California sources, including your income for services performed in California.

Example 2 – In December 2020, you moved to California on an indefinite job assignment. You rented an apartment in California and continued to live in the apartment. You retained your home and bank account in Illinois until April 2021, at which time you sold your home and transferred your bank account to California.

Determination: Your assignment in California was for an indefinite period; therefore, your stay in California was not of a temporary or transitory nature. Although you kept ties in Illinois until April 2021, you became a California resident upon entering the state in December 2020. As a resident, you are taxed on your income from all sources.

Leaving California

Any individual who is a resident of California continues to be a resident when absent from the state for a temporary or transitory purpose.

An absence from California under an employment-related contract for a period of at least 546 consecutive days may be considered an absence for other than a temporary or transitory purpose. See "Safe Harbor" on page 4 for more information.

Example 3 – Until September 2021, you were a resident of California. At that time, you declared yourself to be a resident of Nevada, where you have a summer home. You continue to spend six or seven months each year at your home in California, which you have retained. You spend only three to four months in Nevada and the rest of the time traveling in other states or countries. You transferred your bank accounts to Nevada. However, you continue to maintain your social club and business connections in California.

Determination: Your declaration of residency in Nevada does not establish residency in that state. Your closest connections are to California and your absence from California is for temporary or transitory purposes. You are, therefore, a resident of California and are taxed on your income from all sources.

Example 4 – You and your spouse/RDP are California residents. You accept a contract to work in South America for 16 months. You lease an apartment near the job site. Your contract states that your employer will arrange your return back to California when your contract expires. Your spouse/RDP and your children will remain in California residing in the home you own.

Determination: You maintain strong ties with California because your spouse/RDP and children remain in your California home during your absence. Your intent is to return to California, and your absence is temporary and transitory. You remain a California resident during your absence. You are taxed on income from all sources, including income earned in South America.

Example 5 – You receive and accept a permanent job offer in Spain. You and your spouse/RDP sell your home in California, pack all of your possessions and move to Spain on May 5, 2021, with your children. You lease an apartment and enroll your children in school in Spain. You obtain a driver's license from Spain and make numerous social connections in your new home. You have no intention of returning to California.

Determination: You are a part-year resident. Through May 4, 2021, you were a California resident. On May 5, 2021, you became a nonresident. All your income while you were a resident is taxable by California. While you are a nonresident, only income from California sources is taxable by California.

Example 6 – You are a resident of California. You accept a 15-month assignment in Saudi Arabia. You put your personal belongings, including your automobile, in storage in California. You have a California driver's license and are registered to vote in California. You maintain bank accounts in California. In Saudi Arabia, you stay in a compound provided for you by your employer, and the only ties you establish there are connected to your employment. Upon completion of your assignment, you will return to California.

Determination: You have maintained greater connections with California than you have established in Saudi Arabia. Your absence is for a temporary or transitory purpose. Therefore, you remain a California resident. As a California resident, your income from all sources is taxable by California, including the income that you earned from your assignment in Saudi Arabia.

Example 7 – You are a resident of California and a single taxpayer. You accept a three-year assignment in Japan. Your assignment in Japan covers the period January 1, 2020, through December 31, 2022. You rented out your residence and put your truck and belongings in storage in California. You maintained your California bank accounts, driver's license, and voter registration. You have less than $200,000 of intangible income during each year. Upon completion of your assignment, you intend to return to California. You returned to California to visit family no longer than a total of 45 days during 2020 or 2021.

Determination: You meet the safe harbor rule. You are a nonresident during your absence from the state.

I Income Taxable by California

Residents of California are taxed on ALL income, including income from sources outside California.

Nonresidents of California are taxed only on income from California sources. Nonresidents of California are not taxed on pensions received after December 31, 1995. For more information, get FTB Pub. 1005, Pension and Annuity Guidelines.

Part-year residents of California are taxed on all income received while a resident and only on income from California sources while a nonresident.

If you use Form 540NR, figure your taxable income as if you were a California resident for the entire year. Complete Schedule CA (540NR), California Adjustments — Nonresidents or Part-Year Residents, column A through column D, to figure total adjusted gross income (AGI). Figure California AGI applicable to a nonresident or part-year resident on Schedule CA (540NR), column E.

Treat specific types of income as explained below.

Wages and Salaries

Wages and salaries have a source where the services are performed. Neither the location of the employer, where the payment is issued, nor your location when you receive payment affect the source of this income. Part-year residents include on Schedule CA (540NR), column E all wages and salaries earned while a resident, regardless of where the services were performed. Nonresidents include the income for services performed in California.

Example 1 – You are a resident of New York working temporarily in California for a New York corporation.

Determination: Your income earned for services performed in California has a California source. As a nonresident, include this California source income on Schedule CA (540NR), column E.

Example 2 – You are a California resident. As a representative for your employer, you spent two weeks in Georgia to give training. You were paid by a Georgia corporation while you were in Georgia.

Determination: Because you are a California resident, you are taxed on all income, regardless of source. The income is taxable by California, even though it has a source in Georgia.

Interest and Dividends

Interest and dividends generally have a source where you are a resident. However, see Exception below.

Example 3 – You are a resident of Texas and have interest from a California bank account.

Determination: Because you are a resident of Texas, the interest has a source in Texas. The interest is not taxable by California.

Example 4 – You are a resident of California and have interest from a savings account in Oregon.

Determination: Because you are a California resident, you are taxed on all income, regardless of source. The interest is taxable by California.

Example 5 – You are a resident of Montana and have dividends from a California corporation.

Determination: Because you are a Montana resident, the dividends have a source in Montana. The dividends are not taxable by California.

Exception: Interest and dividends have a source in California if the account or security is used in a trade or business or pledged as security for a loan, the proceeds of which are used in a trade or business in California. For special rules regarding qualifying investment securities, refer to California Revenue and Taxation Code (R&TC) Section 17955.

Business Income (or Loss)

A nonresident's income from California sources includes income from a business, trade, or profession carried on in California. If the nonresident's business, trade, or profession is carried on both within and outside California, the income sourced to California may be based only on the business conducted within California, or may be determined by using the apportionment formula for corporations engaged in multistate businesses.

California uses a mandatory market assignment method and single-sales factor apportionment to apportion business income to California. A nonresident may have California sourced income or apportionable business income if receiving income from sales or services sourced to California. Such income includes:

1. Sales of services to the extent that the purchaser of the service receives the benefit of the service in California.
2. Sales of intangible property to the extent that the intangible property is used in California. For marketable securities, the sales are in California if the customer is in California.
3. Sales from the sale, lease, rental, or licensing of real property if the real property is located in California.
4. Sales from the rental, lease, or licensing of tangible personal property if the property is located in California.

Refer to Cal. Code Regs., tit.18 section 17951-4 to determine when income from business, trade or profession should be sourced according to apportionment rules. Also see R&TC Section 25136 and Cal. Code Regs., tit. 18 section 25136-2 or California Schedule R, Apportionment and Allocation of Income, for more information.

Withholding may be required on a nonresident's business income if an exemption, waiver, or reduction is not certified or approved.

Pensions and Keoghs

Residents: Distributions from employer-sponsored and self-employment (Keogh) pension, profit-sharing, stock bonus plans, or other deferred compensation arrangements are taxable by California regardless of where the services were performed.

Nonresidents: Distributions are not taxable by California if received after December 31, 1995. Get FTB Pub. 1005 for more information.

Example 6 – You were a resident of California when you earned your pension. You retired during 2021 and moved permanently to New Mexico. After becoming a resident of New Mexico, you begin drawing your pension.

Determination: Since you are a nonresident, the distribution is not taxable by California because you received it after December 31, 1995.

Example 7 – You lived and worked in Ohio. You retired in Ohio and received your first pension check on January 1, 2021. You moved permanently to California on July 1, 2021.

Determination: You became a California resident on July 1, 2021. Your pension income received beginning July 1, 2021, is taxable by California because California residents are taxed on all income, regardless of source.

Lump-Sum Distributions

Residents: Lump-sum distributions are taxable by California. Residents of California are taxed on all income, regardless of source. Therefore, the distribution is taxable even if it is attributable to services performed outside of California and accrued prior to your becoming a California resident.

Nonresidents: Lump-sum distributions from a qualified plan or annuity after December 31, 1995, are not taxable by California. However, lump-sum distributions, derived from a California source, received from most nonqualified plans after December 31, 1995, continue to be taxable by California. For more information, get FTB Pub. 1005.

Example 8 – You lived and worked in New York. You retired and moved to California and became a resident. Prior to relocating, you elected to receive a lump-sum distribution from your qualified pension plan. You received the distribution after you became a California resident.

Determination: The distribution is taxable by California because California residents are taxed on all income, regardless of source (Appeal of Ralph G. and Martha E. McQuoid, California State Board of Equalization, May 11, 1989).

Example 9 – You were a California resident and worked for a corporation in California. You moved to Ohio during 2021 and elected to take a lump-sum distribution from your qualified pension plan. You received the distribution after you became a resident of Ohio.

Determination: Since you are a nonresident, the distribution is **not** taxable by California because you received it after December 31, 1995.

Individual Retirement Account (IRA), Roth IRA, SIMPLE IRA, Simplified Employee Pension (SEP), and Keogh Distributions

IRA, Roth IRA, SIMPLE IRA, SEP, and Keogh distributions received after becoming a nonresident are not taxable by California if received after December 31, 1995.

Distributions from an SEP from contributions made after 1986 are taxed by California in the same manner as pension and Keogh distributions. Distributions from contributions made before 1987 are taxed by California in the same manner as IRA distributions. For more information, get FTB Pub. 1005.

Sale of Real Estate

The gain or loss from the sale of real estate has a source where the property is located. If you sell your California real estate and move out of state, the gain is taxable by California. The gain is taxable by California even if the real estate is sold when you are a nonresident.

Example 10 – You are a resident of Idaho. You sold undeveloped real estate located in California at a gain.

Determination: Because the property is in California, the gain is California source income. As a nonresident, include this California source income on Schedule CA (540NR), column E.

Example 11 – You are a resident of California. You sold real estate located in England at a gain.

Determination: Because you are a California resident, you are taxed on all income, regardless of source. The gain on the sale is taxable by California.

Example 12 – You are a resident of Nevada. You own residential rental property located in California. Your property has always shown a loss. You sold the property for a gain.

Determination: Because the property is located in California, the gain on the sale is taxable by California. Since rental real property is classified as a passive activity, the sale "triggers" the release of suspended losses incurred in taxable years beginning on or after January 1, 1987. The suspended losses may be used to offset any gain from the sale or income from other passive activities. For more information, get form FTB 3801, Passive Activity Loss Limitations, and instructions, or FTB Pub. 1016, Real Estate Withholding Guidelines.

Withholding Services and Compliance

Withholding may be required on income with a California source. This includes, sales of California real estate, income allocations or distributions from S corporations and partnerships, and other payments of California source income paid to nonresidents. **Note:** Withholding is not always required. An exemption, reduction, or waiver can be filed.

With certain limited exceptions, payers that are required to withhold and remit backup withholding to the Internal Revenue Service (IRS) are also required to withhold and remit to the FTB. The California backup withholding rate is 7% of the payment. For California purposes, dividends, interests, and any financial institution's release of loan funds made in the normal course of business are exempt from backup withholding. For additional information on California backup withholding, go to **ftb.ca.gov** and search for **backup withholding**.

For more information regarding California withholding requirements, get FTB Pub. 1016 and Pub. 1017, Resident and Nonresident Withholding Guidelines.

Write to:

WITHHOLDING SERVICES AND COMPLIANCE
MS F182
FRANCHISE TAX BOARD
PO BOX 942867
SACRAMENTO CA 94267-0651

Telephone:	**888**.792.4900 from within the United States 916.845.4900 from outside the United States
California Relay Service:	711 or 800.735.2929 for persons with hearing or speaking limitations
FAX:	916.845.9512

Partnership, S Corporation, Limited Liability Company (LLC), and Trust Income (Loss)

When a partner is a part-year resident during any part of the partner's or the partnership's taxable year, the part-year resident must divide his or her taxable year into two distinct periods. For the period during which the part-year resident was a resident of this state, all items of income and deductions are to be included in the partner's California taxable income. For the period during which the part-year resident was a nonresident of this state, only gross income and deductions realized from sources within this state are included in the partner's California taxable income. Therefore, all California-sourced items of income and loss realized by the partnership during the partnership's taxable year when the partner was a nonresident of this state are included in California taxable income. This also applies to shareholders of an S corporation, partners of an LLC classified as a partnership, and beneficiaries of a trust. See FTB Legal Ruling 2003-1, FTB Pub. 1017, and FTB Pub. 1100 for more information.

Example 13 – Kim, a nonresident calendar year individual taxpayer, has a 50% interest in partnership (P). P has a December 31 year-end. P conducts business within and outside California. For the fiscal year ended December 31, Kim's Schedule K-1 (565), Partner's Share of Income, Deductions, Credits, etc., from P shows that Kim has $10,000 of taxable income from all sources, $5,000 of which is sourced to California. On September 15, Kim became a resident of California.

Determination: Kim was a nonresident for 257 days of P's fiscal year and a resident for 108 days. Kim will include in California taxable income for the year, $6,480 of income from P, computed as follows:

- For the portion of the year Kim was a nonresident: 257/365 X $ 5,000 = $3,521
- For the portion of the year Kim was a resident: 108/365 X $10,000 = $2,959

Example 14 – Hope, a calendar year individual resident of California, owns a 50% share of an S corporation (Buddy Corp.). Buddy Corp. has an October 31 year-end. Buddy Corp. conducts business within and outside California. For the October 31 year-end, Hope's Schedule K-1 (100S), Shareholder's Share of Income, Deductions, Credits, etc., from Buddy Corp. shows that Hope has $8,000 of taxable income from all sources, $3,000 of which is sourced to California. On June 10, Hope became a nonresident taxpayer.

Determination: Hope was a nonresident for 144 days of Buddy Corp.'s fiscal year-end and a resident for 221 days. Hope will include in California taxable income for the year, $6,028 of income from Buddy Corp., computed as follows:

- For the portion of the year Hope was a nonresident: 144/365 X $3,000 = $1,184
- For the portion of the year Hope was a resident: 221/365 X $8,000 = $4,844

Sale of Stocks and Bonds

The gain or loss from the sale of stocks or bonds has a source where you are a resident at the time of the sale. If buying and selling stocks and bonds is your trade or business, see "Business Income (or Loss)" on page 7 for more information.

Example 15 – You are a resident of Oregon and sell stock of a California corporation at a gain.

Determination: Because you are an Oregon resident, the gain has an Oregon source. The gain is not taxable by California.

Example 16 – You are a resident of California and sell stock of a Kansas corporation at a gain.

Determination: Because you are a California resident, you are taxed on all income, regardless of source. The gain is taxable by California.

Installment Sales

California taxes installment gains received by a nonresident from the sale of tangible property on a source basis. Real property is sourced and taxed based upon where the property is located. California taxes residents on all income regardless of source. The chart below indicates the tax treatment for installment payments received by residents, nonresidents, and individuals who changed residency:

Residency Status	Sold Property	California Property	Out-of-State Property
Always a Nonresident	Anytime	Taxable	Nontaxable
Always a Resident	Anytime	Taxable	Taxable
Former Resident	Prior to moving out	Taxable	2001 and prior - Taxable
			2002 and after - Nontaxable
Former Nonresident	Prior to moving in	Taxable	2001 and prior - Nontaxable
			2002 and after - Taxable

For the treatment of interest earned on an installment sale, see "Interest and Dividends" on page 7.

For more information regarding the taxation of installment sales, get FTB Pub. 1100.

Reimbursement of Moving Expenses

The source of reimbursed moving expenses is the state to which you move, regardless of your residency at the time the reimbursement is made.

J Specific Professions

Military and Spouses

Military personnel and spouses should get FTB Pub. 1032.

Civilians Working for the Military

The rules for military personnel do not apply to civilians working for the military. Determine your residency status and the source of your income based on the guidelines previously explained in Sections E through I.

Career Appointees in the U.S. Foreign Service

The rules for military personnel and spouses do not apply to career appointees in the U.S. Foreign Service. Determine your residency status and the source of your income based on the guidelines previously explained in Sections E through I.

Airline Employees

The wages of nonresident flight personnel (e.g. pilot, copilot, flight attendant) are not taxable by California unless more than 50% of the individual's scheduled flight time is in California. If more than 50% of the scheduled flight time is in California, wages are apportioned to California based on the ratio of time spent in California to the total scheduled flight time.

Flight personnel who are California residents are taxed on all wages received regardless of where the flight time is spent.

Interstate Rail and Motor Carrier Employees

The wages of nonresident railroad employees or truck drivers whose regularly assigned duties are performed in two or more states may only be taxed by the individual's state of residence.

Railroad employees or truck drivers who are California residents are taxed on all wages received regardless of where the duties are performed.

Merchant Seamen

A merchant seaman who is in California only because this state is a port-of-call and who maintains no other contact or connections with this state, is a nonresident. However, a seaman who maintains close connections with California remains a California resident while at sea. Under such circumstances, the seaman's absence is for a temporary or transitory purpose.

Example 1 – You are a merchant seaman and spend six to ten months a year aboard a ship outside California. You spend your off-duty time in California. You own a home in California where your spouse/RDP resides. You vote and bank in California. You have a California driver's license and your automobile is registered in California.

Determination: You are a resident of California. Your time at sea is temporary and transitory. As a resident, all your income is taxable by California, including your income earned while at sea (Appeal of James H. and Leila P. Pike, California State Board of Equalization, February 1, 1983).

Example 2 – You are a merchant seaman and spend eight to ten months a year aboard a ship outside California. You are single and have no dependents. You spend 50% of your off-duty time or 10% of your total time in California. You return to California only when your employment brings you here. When visiting California, you stay in hotels. You have a California bank account in joint tenancy with your father. You have a California driver's license, but no car. You do not own real property in California.

Determination: You are a nonresident of California. Your ties to California are not substantial and your time in California is temporary or transitory (Appeal of Richard W. Vohs, California State Board of Equalization, September 17, 1973).

K Residents of or Individuals in Foreign Countries

If you are a resident of a foreign country and perform services in California and/or receive income from California sources, you may have a California income tax filing requirement even if you do not have a federal filing requirement.

Tax Treaty

A tax treaty between the U.S. Government and a foreign country may exempt some types of income from federal taxation. Generally, unless the treaty specifically excludes the income from taxation by California, the income is taxable.

Example 1 – You are a resident of China doing research at a university in California and received wages of $15,000 for teaching and doing research. For federal income tax purposes, the wages are excludable due to the tax treaty between the United States and China.

Amounts received for teaching, research, or other services performed by a student are not excludable as a qualified scholarship or fellowship, even if the services are required as a condition of receiving the scholarship or fellowship.

Determination: Although the wages may be exempt from income for federal income tax purposes, the wages will be taxable by California. The tax treaty specifically states that the taxes covered by the tax treaty are federal income taxes imposed by the Internal Revenue Code. Tax treaties between the United States and other countries which expressly limit their application to federal income taxes do not apply to California. Nonresidents are taxed by California on wages for services performed in California. Since you received wages for services performed in California, the wages are taxable by California. Include the wages of $15,000 on Schedule CA (540NR), Part II, Section A, line 1, column C.

Income Tax Clearance

A federal income tax clearance does not affect your California tax liability. The FTB does not issue tax clearance certificates for individuals in this situation.

Foreign Tax Credit or Foreign Earned Income Exclusion

California does not allow a foreign tax credit or a foreign earned income exclusion. If you claimed the foreign earned income exclusion on your federal return, include the amount of your foreign earned income exclusion on Schedule CA (540NR), Part II, Section B, line 8d, column C.

L Meaning of Domicile

The term "domicile" has a special legal definition that is not the same as residence. While many states consider domicile and residence to be the same, California makes a distinction and views them as two separate concepts, even though they may often overlap. For instance, you may be domiciled in California but not be a California resident or you may be domiciled in another state but be a California resident for income tax purposes.

Domicile is defined for tax purposes as the place where you voluntarily establish yourself and family, not merely for a special or limited purpose, but with a present intention of making it your true, fixed, permanent home and principal establishment. It is the place where, whenever you are absent, you intend to return. The maintenance of a marital abode in California is a significant factor in establishing domicile in California.

Change of Domicile

You can have only one domicile at a time. Once you acquire a domicile, you retain that domicile until you acquire another.

A change of domicile requires all of the following:

- Abandonment of your prior domicile.
- Physically moving to and residing in the new locality.
- Intent to remain in the new locality permanently or indefinitely as demonstrated by your actions.

M Married/RDP Filing Separate Returns

Division of Income

California is a community property state. The domicile of the spouse/RDP earning the income determines the division of income between spouses/RDPs when separate returns are filed. Each spouse/RDP must follow the laws in his or her state of domicile to determine whether income is separate or community. When separate returns are filed, you and your spouse/RDP must each report half of the community income plus all of your separate income on your return. See Section L, Meaning of Domicile.

Community Property

Community property is all of the property that is not separate property acquired by a husband/RDP or wife/RDP or both while domiciled in a community property state, U.S. territory, or country.

Each spouse/RDP owns one-half of all community property. If property cannot be specifically identified as separate property, it is considered community property.

The following are community property states and U.S. territories (countries not listed):

Arizona	New Mexico
California	Northern Mariana Islands
Guam	Puerto Rico
Idaho	Texas
Louisiana	Washington
Nevada	Wisconsin

Community Income

Income generated from community property is community income. Community income also includes compensation for services if the spouse/RDP earning the compensation is domiciled in a community property state.

Divide the community income equally between you and your spouse/RDP when separate returns are filed.

Separate Property

Separate property includes the following:

- Property owned separately by each spouse/RDP before marriage or registering as a domestic partnership.
- Property received separately as gifts or inheritances.
- Property purchased with separate property funds.
- Money earned while domiciled in a separate property state.
- All property declared separate property in a valid agreement.

Maintain separate property separately. If the property or the income from the property is used for community purposes, or commingled, it could lose its separate property character, overriding any agreements.

Separate Income

Generally, income from separate property is income of the spouse/RDP who owns the property. When filing, you and your spouse/RDP report your income(s) separately on your separate returns.

Deductions

Expenses incurred to earn or produce community business or investment income are generally divided equally between you and your spouse/RDP. Each spouse/RDP is entitled to deduct half of the expenses of the business or investment expenses on his or her separate return.

Expenses incurred to earn or produce separate business or investment income are deductible by the spouse/RDP who owns the investment generating the income, provided that spouse/RDP pays the expenses from his or her separate funds.

Expenses that are not attributable to any specific income, such as medical expenses, are deductible by the spouse/RDP who pays them. If these expenses are paid from community funds, the deduction is divided equally between you and your spouse/RDP.

If one spouse/RDP itemizes deductions, both spouses/RDPs must itemize deductions, even if the itemized deductions of one spouse/RDP are less than the standard deduction.

Exemption Credits

When you file separate returns, you and your spouse/RDP must each claim your own personal exemption credit.

When you have more than one dependent supported by community funds, you and your spouse/RDP may divide the number of dependents between you in any manner you choose. However, you may not split the credit for any one dependent.

Division of Income, Residents and Nonresidents of California – Examples

Example 1 – You and your spouse/RDP are residents of California. You earned $15,000 in wages. Your spouse/RDP earned $30,000. In addition to wages, you have stock that you inherited. The stock is in your name only, and you keep the stock and the dividend income separate from community funds. You received $5,000 in dividends. You have decided to file separate returns.

Determination: You and your spouse/RDP each have $22,500 in community income: ($15,000 + $30,000 = $45,000 ÷ 2). In addition to your $22,500 in community income to be reported, include the $5,000 of separate income from dividends, making your total income $27,500.

Example 2 – You and your spouse/RDP are residents of California. For the first six months of the year, you earned wages of $30,000. Your spouse/RDP did not earn any income. On June 30, you and your spouse/RDP physically separated with no intention of reconciliation. During the last six months, you earned wages of $30,000 and your spouse/RDP earned wages of $10,000. You have decided to file separate returns.

Determination: For the first six months of the year, your earnings were community income. You and your spouse/RDP must each report on your individual returns one half of the income earned during this period. When you and your spouse/RDP physically separated with no intention of reconciliation, your community income status ended. Therefore, from July 1 through December 31, the income earned by you and your spouse/RDP was separate income.

	You	Your Spouse/RDP
Community		
Jan.–June	$15,000	$15,000
Separate		
July–Dec.	30,000	10,000
Total	$45,000	$25,000

Example 3:

John and Jackie are full-year nonresidents of California. Jackie earned $30,000 in wages for services performed in her state of residence. Jackie also sold property in California that was her separate property. She had a $100,000** gain. John received a pension distribution of $10,000 in 2021 based on services performed in California. For California purposes, John's taxable pension distribution for the year is 0.* John has a rental house in California that is his separate property. His net rental income was $1,000.** John and Jackie filed separate federal returns, therefore, they file separate California returns. The following situations show how their income should be divided based on domicile.

1. John and Jackie are both domiciled in community property states.		John		Jackie	
	TOTAL	Schedule CA (540NR), column D	Schedule CA (540NR), column E	Schedule CA (540NR), column D	Schedule CA (540NR), column E
WAGES	$ 30,000	$ 15,000	$ 0	$ 15,000	$ 0
GAIN	100,000	0	0	100,000	100,000
PENSION	10,000	5,000	0	5,000	0
RENTAL INCOME	1,000	1,000	1,000	0	0

John would complete his Schedule CA (540NR) as shown in the partial view that follows.

Part II **Income Adjustment Schedule**	A	B	C	D	E
Section A — Income from federal Form 1040 or 1040-SR	**Federal Amounts** (taxable amounts from your federal tax return)	**Subtractions** See instructions (difference between CA and federal law)	**Additions** See instructions (difference between CA and federal law)	**Total Amounts Using CA Law As If You Were a CA Resident** (subtract col. B from col. A; add col. C to the result)	**CA Amounts** (income earned or received as a CA resident and income earned or received from CA sources as a nonresident)
1 Wages, salaries, tips, etc. See instructions before making an entry in col. B or C 1	$15,000			$15,000	
5 Pensions and annuities. See instructions a $10,000 . . . . 5b	5,000			5,000	
Section B — Additional Income from federal Schedule 1 (Form 1040)					
5 Rental real estate, royalties, partnerships, S corporations, trusts, etc. 5	1,000			1,000	1,000

*California nonresidents are **not** taxed by California on pension income.

**This income is from separate property; therefore, it is not divided even when domiciled in a community property state.

2. John and Jackie are domiciled in separate property states.		John		Jackie	
	TOTAL	Schedule CA (540NR), column D	Schedule CA (540NR), column E	Schedule CA (540NR), column D	Schedule CA (540NR), column E
WAGES	$ 30,000	$ 0	$ 0	$ 30,000	$ 0
GAIN	100,000	0	0	100,000	100,000
PENSION	10,000	10,000	0	0	0
RENTAL INCOME	1,000	1,000	1,000	0	0

3. John is domiciled in a community property state and Jackie in a separate property state.		John		Jackie	
	TOTAL	Schedule CA (540NR), column D	Schedule CA (540NR), column E	Schedule CA (540NR), column D	Schedule CA (540NR), column E
WAGES	$ 30,000	$ 0	$ 0	$ 30,000	$ 0
GAIN	100,000	0	0	100,000	100,000
PENSION	10,000	5,000	0	5,000	0
RENTAL INCOME	1,000	1,000	1,000	0	0

4. John is domiciled in a separate property state and Jackie in a community property state.		John		Jackie	
	TOTAL	Schedule CA (540NR), column D	Schedule CA (540NR), column E	Schedule CA (540NR), column D	Schedule CA (540NR), column E
WAGES	$ 30,000	$15,000	$ 0	$ 15,000	$ 0
GAIN	100,000	0	0	100,000	100,000
PENSION	10,000	10,000	0	0	0
RENTAL INCOME	1,000	1,000	1,000	0	0

How To Split Income on Form 540NR

Use this chart as a guide to split community income with your spouse/RDP based on domicile if you are married/RDP and file Form 540NR.

Reminder: Include all of your separate income in addition to your half of the community income when filing. See "Division of Income" on pages 10, 11, and 12.

TYPE	YOUR DOMICILE	YOUR SPOUSE'S/RDP's DOMICILE	Form 540NR, Married/RDP Filing Jointly	Form 540NR, Married/RDP Filing Separately (you)	Form 540NR, Married/RDP Filing Separately (your spouse's/RDP's)
1	Community Property State	Community Property State	Schedule CA (540NR), column A through column D: All income All deductions	Schedule CA (540NR), column A through column D: Half of all income Half of all deductions	Schedule CA (540NR), column A through column D: Half of all income Half of all deductions
			Schedule CA (540NR), column E: All income taxable by California	Schedule CA (540NR), column E: Half of all income taxable by California	Schedule CA (540NR), column E: Half of all income taxable by California
2	Separate Property State	Separate Property State	Schedule CA (540NR), column A through column D: All income All deductions	Schedule CA (540NR), column A through column D: All your income All your deductions	Schedule CA (540NR), column A through column D: All your spouse's/RDP's income All your spouse's/RDP's deductions
			Schedule CA (540NR), column E: All income taxable by California	Schedule CA (540NR), column E: All your income taxable by California	Schedule CA (540NR), column E: All your spouse's/RDP's income taxable by California
3	Community Property State	Separate Property State	Schedule CA (540NR), column A through column D: All income All deductions	Schedule CA (540NR), column A through column D: Half of your income Half of your deductions	Schedule CA (540NR), column A through column D: All your spouse's/RDP's income plus half of your income All your spouse's/RDP's deductions plus half of your deductions
			Schedule CA (540NR), column E: All income taxable by California	Schedule CA (540NR), column E: Half of your income taxable by California	Schedule CA (540NR), column E: All your spouse's/RDP's income taxable by California plus half of your income taxable by California
4	Separate Property State	Community Property State	Schedule CA (540NR), column A through column D: All income All deductions	Schedule CA (540NR), column A through column D: All your income plus half of your spouse's/RDP's income All your deductions plus half of your spouse's/RDP's deductions	Schedule CA (540NR), column A through column D: Half of your spouse's/RDP's income Half of your spouse's/RDP's deductions
			Schedule CA (540NR), column E: All income taxable by California	Schedule CA (540NR), column E: All your income taxable by California plus half of your spouse's/RDP's income taxable by California	Schedule CA (540NR), column E: Half of your spouse's/RDP's income taxable by California

For information on income taxable by California, see Section I on page 6.

N Avoid Common Mistakes on Form 540NR

Avoid making time-consuming and costly mistakes by reporting your AGI from all sources as if you were a resident of California for the entire year.

California tax returns start with federal AGI. However, there are differences between California and federal tax law. Use Schedule CA (540NR) to convert your federal AGI (column A) to your total AGI from all sources under California law (column D) as follows:

- Copy your federal income, adjustments, and deductions to the applicable lines on Schedule CA (540NR), column A.
- Subtract income that is taxable under federal law but not under California law (such as California lottery winnings and social security benefits) by entering it on Schedule CA (540NR), column B.
- Add income excluded on the federal return (such as foreign income or income from non-California municipal bonds), unless the income is specifically excludable under California law, by entering it on Schedule CA (540NR), column C.
- **Do not** subtract non-California source income to determine your total AGI from all sources under California law.

When you figure your California AGI on Schedule CA (540NR), column E, be sure to include the following:

- All income from every source while you were a resident of California.
- Income from California sources while you were a nonresident.

For more information, get the instructions for Schedule CA (540NR).

O Double-Taxed Income

If you paid taxes to California and to another state on the same income, you may qualify for a tax credit for taxes paid to another state. Get California Schedule S, Other State Tax Credit.

P General Phone Service

Telephone assistance is available year-round from 7 a.m. until 5 p.m. Monday through Friday, except holidays. Hours subject to change.

Telephone:	800.852.5711 from within the United States 916.845.6500 from outside the United States
California Relay Service:	711 or 800.735.2929 for persons with hearing or speaking limitations
IRS:	800.829.1040 for federal tax questions, call the IRS

Asistencia En Español

Asistencia telefónica está disponible durante todo el año desde las 7 a.m. hasta las 5 p.m. de lunes a viernes, excepto días feriados. Las horas están sujetas a cambios.

Teléfono:	800.852.5711 dentro de los Estados Unidos 916.845.6500 fuera de los Estados Unidos
Servicio de Retransmisión de California:	711 o 800.735.2929 para personas con limitaciones auditivas o del habla
IRS:	800.829.1040 para preguntas sobre impuestos federales, llame al IRS

Exhibit "D"

OFFICE OF TAX APPEALS

STATE OF CALIFORNIA

In the Matter of the Appeal of:	) OTA Case No. 18010932
J. BRACAMONTE AND	)
J. BRACAMONTE	)

OPINION

Representing the Parties:

For Appellants:	Gregory S. Markow, Attorney Phillip L. Jelsma, Attorney
For Respondent:	Ronald Hofsdal, Tax Counsel IV Desiree Macedo, Tax Counsel
For Office of Tax Appeals:	Neha Garner, Tax Counsel III

R. TAY, Administrative Law Judge: Pursuant to Revenue and Taxation Code (R&TC) section 19045, J. Bracamonte and J. Bracamonte (appellants) appeal an action by Franchise Tax Board (respondent) proposing $1,592,648 of additional tax and applicable interest for the 2008 tax year, and $50,337 of additional tax, a late filing penalty of $12,584.25, and applicable interest for the 2009 tax year.

Office of Tax Appeals Administrative Law Judges Richard Tay, John O. Johnson, and Huy "Mike" Le held an oral hearing on December 14, 2020.[1] At the conclusion of the hearing, we closed the record and submitted this matter for decision.

ISSUE[2]

Whether appellants were California residents on July 18, 2008, such that the proceeds from the sale of Jimsair Aviation Services, Inc. (Jimsair) are subject to California taxation.

[1] The oral hearing was noticed for Sacramento, California, and conducted electronically due to COVID-19.

[2] At the oral hearing, appellants clarified their position on the late filing penalty, which is that the penalty must be abated only if they prevail on the residency issue. Appellants made no additional argument at the hearing to support abatement of the penalty. Since, as discussed below, appellants have not prevailed on the residency issue, the late filing penalty will not be abated and, consequently, we do not address this issue further.

FACTUAL FINDINGS

1. Appellants, a married couple, lived in and were residents of California through 2007. Appellants, individually and/or through their family trust, owned all the outstanding shares of Jimsair, a corporation.
2. Appellants purchased a California home, which they owned from 1988 through December 2017.[3]
3. On February 25, 2008, appellants drove to Henderson, Nevada, and stayed for three days (February 25 to February 27) at a hotel or motel. While in Henderson, appellants looked for an apartment to rent and secured an apartment on February 26, 2008.
4. During their three-day stay in Henderson, appellants obtained a post office box and set up the option to have their mail forwarded to them.[4] Appellants also registered to vote in Nevada and obtained Nevada driver's licenses. Appellant-husband obtained a cell phone number with a Nevada area code, and appellants also opened new Wells Fargo bank accounts in Henderson, Nevada.
5. After their three-day stay, appellants traveled to their property in Lake Havasu City, Arizona, and stayed for one day (February 28). On that day, they changed the address of their preexisting Wells Fargo account to reflect their Nevada mailing address.
6. On March 6, 2008, appellants took possession of the apartment in Henderson, Nevada. The initial rental period ran from March 1, 2008, to August 31, 2008; however, appellants later extended the rental period to September 30, 2008.
7. On the same day they took possession of the apartment, appellants updated their mailing address for a life insurance policy to reflect their new Henderson, Nevada address. Appellant-husband also had an eye exam in Nevada. Later, on March 21, 2008, appellants had their Chevrolet Avalanche serviced at a Jiffy Lube located in Henderson, Nevada. Later, in May, appellants registered their Chevrolet Avalanche in Nevada.

---

[3] Appellants assert that when they moved from California to Nevada in February 2008, they did not make immediate arrangements to sell their California home due to the economic recession, their need to continue caring for appellant-wife's father, who passed away in September 2016, and appellant-husband's focus on starting a new business in Nevada. Appellants assert that they put their California home on the market in April 2015, but as of December 15, 2017, it had not sold, even though appellants had reduced the asking price a number of times.

[4] Appellant-husband testified that appellants had the post office forward their mail to Montana a few times in 2008 while on lengthy travels in their motorhome, but never to California.

8. On March 22, 2008, appellants attended a real estate auction in Las Vegas; however, they did not find a house to purchase at that auction.
9. On April 2, 2008, appellants hired The Rushforth Firm in Nevada and paid them a $1,000 retainer to change their family trust from a California trust to a Nevada trust.
10. Two days later, on April 4, 2008, appellants purchased a trailer in Nevada and later registered the trailer in Nevada on May 13, 2008.
11. In May 2008, appellants purchased a 2008 Harley Davidson motorcycle in California and arranged for the motorcycle to be delivered directly to Arizona as an out-of-state purchase. They did not take possession of it in California. Appellants assert that they also relocated and re-registered an electric cart from California to Arizona.
12. In or around May 2008, appellants hired Jim Robertson, a real estate broker in Henderson, Nevada, to help appellants find a house. In the summer of 2008, appellants made offers to buy three different houses, but none of their offers were accepted.
13. From February 25, 2008, through July 18, 2008, appellants made numerous trips between their properties in California, Arizona, and Nevada. In total, from February 25, 2008, through July 18, 2008, appellants spent 28 days in Henderson, Nevada, 90 days at their property in Escondido, California, and 19 days at their property in Lake Havasu City, Arizona.

Sale of Jimsair

14. Appellants testified that in May 2008, they first learned of an opportunity to sell Jimsair. The buyer contacted appellant-husband in May, and a week later, appellants met the buyer in San Diego.
15. The buyer agreed to purchase Jimsair, and on June 2 and June 11, 2008, appellants executed various closing documents in Henderson, Nevada, for the sale of Jimsair.
16. The sale of Jimsair closed on July 18, 2008. The proceeds from the sale they received in the 2008 tax year were deposited into their Wells Fargo account in Nevada. As a result of the sale of Jimsair, appellants received $16,699,000 in 2008 and $617,522 in 2009.

Events Following the Sale of Jimsair

17. On or around July 23, 2008, appellants terminated their post office box in Escondido, California.

18. Appellants registered three vehicles (1999 Yahama XL1200, 2005 Yahama FX Cruiser, and 2005 Zieman watercraft trailer) in Arizona on August 22, 2008.[5]
19. Subsequently, on September 22, 2008, appellants closed on the purchase of a home in Henderson, Nevada.
20. For the 2008 tax year, appellants received Forms W-2 from Jimsair, reporting wage income.[6]
21. From July 18, 2008, through December 31, 2008, appellants made numerous trips between their properties in California, Arizona, and Nevada. In total, from July 18, 2008 through December 31, 2008, appellants spent 72 days in Nevada, 24 days at their property in Escondido, California, and 25 days at their property in Lake Havasu City in Arizona.

Procedural Background

22. Appellants filed FTB Form 540NR for the 2008 tax year. Appellants did not file a timely California income tax return for the 2009 tax year.
23. Respondent audited appellants' 2008 and 2009 tax years and issued Notices of Proposed Assessment (NPAs). Appellants protested the NPAs, and respondent issued Notices of Action affirming the NPAs.
24. Appellants filed this timely appeal.

DISCUSSION

Burden of Proof

FTB's determinations of residency are presumptively correct, and the taxpayer bears the burden of showing error in those determinations. (*Appeal of Mazer,* 2020-OTA-263P.) This presumption is a rebuttable one and will support a finding only in the absence of sufficient evidence to the contrary. (*Appeals of Seltzer, et al.* (80-SBE-154) 1980 WL 5068.) Respondent's determinations cannot, however, be successfully rebutted when the taxpayer fails

---

[5] It is noteworthy that appellants maintained California motor vehicle registrations for these three vehicles as of July 18, 2008. According to California Department of Motor Vehicle records, appellants also maintained California motor vehicle registrations for the following: a 2003 Jeep Grand Cherokee, 2001 Chrysler GEM 825, 1998 Monaco Dynasty, 1997 Yamaha YVZ350, 1999 Yamaha XL1200, 2005 Yamaha FX Cruiser, 2005 Ziema, 1995 TXBRG, 2000 SPCNS, 2003 Polaris, and 2004 Yamaha YZ-250.

[6] Appellants assert that they stopped receiving salaries from Jimsair on or around February 29, 2008.

to present credible, competent, and relevant evidence as to the issues in dispute. (*Ibid.*) Unsupported assertions are insufficient to satisfy a taxpayer's burden of proof. (*Appeal of Magidow* (82-SBE-274) 1982 WL 11930.)

Taxation of Residents

R&TC section 17041(a)(1) provides, in pertinent part, that a tax shall be imposed for each taxable year upon the entire taxable income of every resident of California who is not a part-year resident. Part-year residents are taxed on their income earned while residents of this state, as well as all income derived from California sources. (R&TC, § 17041(b), (i).) R&TC section 17014(a) provides that the term "resident" includes: (1) every individual who is in California for other than a temporary or transitory purpose; and (2) every individual domiciled in California who is outside California for a temporary or transitory purpose. Thus, an individual domiciled in California remains a resident until he or she leaves for other than a temporary or transitory purpose. (See also Cal. Code Regs., tit. 18, § 17014.)

In this appeal, the dispute over appellants' residency is focused on a single transaction – the sale of Jimsair on July 18, 2008. The result of the dispute controls whether appellants must pay California income tax on the net gain from appellants' sale. (See R&TC, § 17041(a)(1).) The parties agree that if appellants are found to be California residents on July 18, 2008, the undisputed date of the sale, the net gain of appellants' sale is taxed in full by California, regardless of whether the income has a source in this state. The parties also agree that if, on the other hand, appellants changed their residency status before July 18, 2008, the proceeds from the sale are not taxable at all by California, because income derived from the sale of intangible property, such as their sale of stock in Jimsair, is sourced to the taxpayer's out-of-state residence, unless the property has acquired a business situs in this state. (R&TC, § 17952.)

Appellants argue that they ceased being residents of California and established their domicile in Nevada on February 26, 2008,[7] the day they secured an apartment in Nevada. After they secured the apartment, and before July 18, 2008, appellants performed a number of changes that actualized their intention to move, including opening a Nevada post office box (to which they forwarded their mail from their California post office box), registering to vote in Nevada,

[7] There was some confusion as to appellants' position regarding the specific date they ceased being California residents. At the oral hearing, appellants clarified their position that February 26, 2008, was the day they ceased being California residents.

obtaining a Nevada cell phone number, establishing care with an eye-care provider, servicing their automobile and purchasing and registering a trailer in Nevada. Appellants also testified to having attended real estate auctions in Las Vegas, Nevada, but they noted they failed to purchase a home before the sale of Jimsair.

To determine appellants' residency, the first question we turn to is whether appellants were domiciled in California. An individual can have only one domicile at any given time. (Cal. Code Regs., tit. 18, § 17014(c).) Domicile is defined as the one location where an individual has the most settled and permanent connection, and the place to which an individual intends to return when absent. (*Appeal of Mazer*, *supra*; Cal. Code Regs., tit. 18, § 17014(c).) An individual who is domiciled in California and leaves the state retains his or her California domicile as long as there is a definite intention of returning to California, regardless of the length of time or the reasons for the absence. (Cal. Code Regs., tit. 18, § 17014(c).) In order to change domicile, a taxpayer must: (1) actually move to a new residence; and (2) intend to remain there permanently or indefinitely. (*Appeal of Mazer*, *supra*; see also *Noble v. Franchise Tax Bd.* (2004) 118 Cal.App.4th 560, 568 [noting these two elements as indispensable to accomplishing a change of domicile].) Intent is not determined merely from unsubstantiated statements; the individual's acts and declarations will also be considered. (*Appeal of Mazer*, *supra*; see also *Noble v. Franchise Tax Bd.*, *supra*, 118 Cal.App.4th at pp. 567-568.)

A domicile, once acquired, is presumed to continue until it is shown to have been changed. (*Appeal of Bailey* (76-SBE-016) 1976 WL 4032.) The burden of proof as to a change of domicile is on the party asserting such change. (*Appeal of Mazer*, *supra*.) If there is doubt on the question of domicile after presentation of the facts and circumstances, then domicile must be found to have not changed. (*Ibid.*)

We find that appellants have not met their burden. To successfully relinquish their California domicile, appellants must have changed their "true, fixed, permanent home and principal establishment, and to which place [they have], whenever [they are] absent, the intention of returning." (Cal. Code Regs., tit. 18, § 17014(c).) Domicile "is the place in which [individuals have] voluntarily fixed the habitation of [themselves and their] family, not for a mere special or limited purpose, but with the present intention of making a permanent home, until some unexpected event shall occur to induce [individuals] to adopt some other permanent home." (*Ibid.*)

It is uncontroverted that appellants had a California domicile prior to 2008. Despite their purported intent to change their California domicile, appellants did not "adopt some other permanent home" when they took possession of their rented apartment in Henderson, Nevada. Rather, their possession of their apartment was marked with impermanence. Appellants rented the apartment in Henderson, Nevada on March 6, 2008, because, as appellant-husband testified at the oral hearing, they "needed a temporary place to live." Appellants testified that, as they looked for a permanent home, they decided to secure an apartment in the area of their desired future home to make purchasing a home easier. Appellants eventually purchased a home in September 2008,[8] but until then, appellants retained their large California home, and left much of their personal property at their California home and spent a majority of their time there from February 25, 2008, through July 18, 2008. Appellants testified that they only took essentials to their Nevada apartment, such as linens, towels, dishes and some basic furniture. Notably, they left their precious mementos and other valuable items in California until they acquired a "permanent home" in Nevada. "In order to change one's domicile, one must actually move to a new residence and intend to remain there permanently or indefinitely." (*Appeal of Berner* (2001-SBE-006-A) 2002 WL 1884256.) Appellants' possession of a rental apartment was part of their plan to find a permanent home, but was not the actual move to a new residence with the intent to remain there permanently. The impermanence of the apartment evidences their intention of returning to their California home until they found a suitable Nevada replacement. Consequently, we find that appellants retained their California domicile through July 18, 2008, and did not change their "permanent home" when they took possession of their apartment.

Since appellants were domiciled in California, we turn to the question of whether appellants were outside California for a temporary or transitory purpose, such that the taxpayer will continue to be treated as a California resident. (R&TC, § 17014(a)(2); Cal. Code Regs., tit. 18, § 17014.) Whether an individual is outside California for a temporary or transitory purpose is a question of fact to be determined by examining all the circumstances of each particular case. (Cal. Code Regs., tit. 18, § 17014(b).) The determination cannot be based solely on the individual's subjective intent but instead must be based on objective facts. (*Appeal of Mazer*, *supra*.)

---

[8] Respondent concedes that appellants changed their domicile to Nevada as of September 29, 2008.

In situations where the taxpayers have significant contacts with more than one state, as appellants do here, the state with the closest connections during the taxable year is the state of residence. (Cal. Code Regs., tit. 18, § 17014(b).) The contacts that taxpayers maintain in this and other states are important objective indications of whether their presence in, or absence from, California was for a temporary or transitory purpose. (*Appeal of Berner*, *supra*.) Such contacts are a measure of the benefits and protection that the taxpayers have received from the laws and government of California and as objective indicia of whether the taxpayers entered or left this state for temporary or transitory purposes. (*Ibid.*)

To evaluate a taxpayer's contacts with a state, *Appeal of Bragg* (2003-SBE-002) 2003 WL 21403264, provides a list of nonexclusive factors that are helpful in determining which state an individual had the closest connection to the period in question. These factors can be separated into three categories: (1) registrations and filings with a state or other agency; (2) personal and professional associations; and (3) physical presence and property. (*Appeal of Mazer*, *supra*.) However, these factors are not exclusive, and serve merely as a guide. (*Ibid.*) The weight given to any particular factor depends upon the totality of the circumstances. (*Ibid.*)

Here, there are numerous relevant connections in California and Nevada that are significant that we will summarize below. We believe appellants' testimony that they were in the process of moving from California to Nevada and establishing residency in Nevada.[9] However, as of July 18, 2008, we find that appellants had not "relinquished . . . their residence in California." (*Noble v. Franchise Tax Bd.*, *supra*, 118 Cal.App.4th at pp. 569.)

Although appellants began to increase their contacts with Nevada, their contacts with California remained significant. Appellants had numerous vehicles and vessels registered in California, including a Harley-Davidson that was purchased in June 2008 and registered in California. Appellants maintained their California post office box address, numerous bank accounts, and established care with healthcare professionals in California. Prior to the sale of Jimsair, appellants conducted business in San Diego, including holding meetings with attorneys about ongoing litigation and meetings that ultimately led to the sale of Jimsair. These connections favor California residency.

---

[9] The record is replete with evidence that appellants' Nevada contacts increased after July 18, 2008. Appellants bought a permanent home, registered more of their vehicles and vessels in Nevada, started a business, voted, and spent most of their time at their new home. However, the relevant date for this appeal is July 18, 2008, and we find subsequent events unpersuasive to the residency determination as of that date.

Most significantly, appellants' physical presence in California from February 26, 2008, the date appellants argue they moved out of California, to July 18, 2008, far outweighed their presence in any other state. As stated above, appellants were in California for 90 days, and in Henderson, Nevada for only 28 days. We find the sheer amount of time spent in California, and the average length of their stay in the respective homes significant.[10] Indeed, physical presence is a factor of greater significance than mental intent and the formalities that tie one to a particular state. (*Noble v. Franchise Tax Bd.*, *supra*, 118 Cal.App.4th at pp. 567; *Whittell v. Franchise Tax Bd.* (1964) 231 Cal.App.2d 278.) Thus, despite appellants' actions to transition to becoming Nevada residents, we find their physical presence in California most persuasive.

Appellants argue that their purpose for being in California after February 25, 2008, was temporary and transitory because they purportedly were in California just to care for family members, and to manage occasional business needs. However, the amount of time appellants spent in California and the breadth of their activities, in addition to the little time they spent actually in Nevada, indicates they were more than just a seasonal visitor to California. (See *Appeal of Berner*, *supra*.) Furthermore, having found appellants remained domiciled in California during the relevant period, the question is not whether they were in California for temporary or transitory purposes, but instead whether they were in a location other than California for other than temporary or transitory purposes. When applying the correct test, the facts show that, contrary to appellants' contention, appellants' time in Nevada is better described as for temporary and transitory purposes.

Since appellants were California domiciliaries and were physically in California for a majority of the time leading up to and on July 18, 2008, we find that appellants' strongest connections were with California. Appellants maintained a permanent home in California, spent the most time in California prior to July 18, 2008, and did not spend much time in Nevada, their purported state of residence. Thus, we find that appellants availed themselves of the benefits and protections of California the most, and consequently, are California residents for tax purposes. Therefore, on the date of the sale of the stock of Jimsair (July 18, 2008), we find that appellants

[10] Between March 6, 2008, when appellants took possession of their apartment, to July 18, 2008, appellants stayed in California an average of 8.5 days at a time. Appellants' stays in Nevada averaged just 2.18 days.

were residents of California and thus subject to personal income tax on the installment sale income received in both 2008 and 2009.[11]

HOLDING

Appellants were California residents on July 18, 2008, and therefore the proceeds from the sale of Jimsair are subject to California taxation.

DISPOSITION

We sustain FTB's action in full.

DocuSigned by:
F8E81582726F448...
Richard Tay
Administrative Law Judge

We concur:

DocuSigned by:
John O Johnson
873D9797B9E64E1...
John O. Johnson
Administrative Law Judge

DocuSigned by:
Huy "Mike" Le
431783ADD49442B...
Huy "Mike" Le
Administrative Law Judge

Date Issued: 3/22/2021

[11] For purposes of the proposed assessment for the 2009 tax year, we do not make a determination of appellants' residency status on any date after July 18, 2008, because even if appellants were nonresidents in 2009, their recognized gain from the installment sale payment they received in 2009 is still sourced to California. (Cal. Code Regs., tit. 18, § 17952(d).)

Exhibit "E"

OFFICE OF TAX APPEALS

STATE OF CALIFORNIA

In the Matter of the Appeal of:	) OTA Case No. 18032402
BLAIR S. BINDLEY	) Date Issued: May 30, 2019

OPINION

Representing the Parties:

For Appellant: Timothy J. DuVall, CPA

For Respondent: Mira Patel, Tax Counsel

For Office of Tax Appeals: Andrea Long, Tax Counsel

P. KUSIAK, Administrative Law Judge: Pursuant to Revenue and Taxation Code (R&TC) section 19045, Blair S. Bindley (appellant) appeals an action by respondent Franchise Tax Board (FTB) affirming its proposed assessment of $532 additional tax, a $135 late-filing penalty, and applicable interest, for the 2015 tax year.

Appellant waived his right to an oral hearing; therefore, the matter is being decided based on the written record.

ISSUE

Whether appellant had taxable income from a California source in 2015.

FACTUAL FINDINGS

1. Appellant is a self-employed screenplay writer providing services to companies producing films and television shows. On or around September 1, 2014, appellant contracted with Mindbender Enterprises, LLC (Mindbender), a motion picture producer, for appellant's writing services to write a screenplay. The contract specifies that appellant's work would be considered "work-for-hire" and Mindbender would therefore be considered the author and copyright owner of appellant's screenplay. On or around December 18, 2015, appellant similarly contracted with Lakeshow Films, LLC

(Lakeshow) to write an original screenplay for the producer. The contract specifies that the screenplay would be considered a "work-made-for-hire" for Lakeshow. Both Mindbender and Lakeshow (collectively, "LLCs") were headquartered and registered in California.

2. FTB annually matches income records obtained from various reporting sources against filed returns to identify individuals who may have not fulfilled their legal requirement to file a California tax return. FTB received information that during 2015, appellant received $25,000 of income from Mindbender and $15,000 of income from Lakeshow. FTB sent appellant a Request for Tax Return (Request) dated May 11, 2017, stating that it had no record of receiving appellant's 2015 return. The Request required appellant to file a 2015 return or explain why he was not required to file a 2015 return. Appellant's response was due by June 14, 2017.

3. FTB received appellant's reply on July 6, 2017. Appellant explained that he did not have California-source income, because he performed all services for Mindbender and Lakeshow in Arizona. During the 2015 tax year, appellant was an Arizona resident.

4. FTB rejected appellant's explanation, because appellant had performed services for California LLCs, and thus, had California-source income. On July 10, 2017, FTB sent appellant a Notice of Proposed Assessment (NPA). The NPA reflected an estimated income of $31,377,[1] deductions of $4,044,[2] and taxable income of $27,333. Based on this estimate, the NPA proposed a total tax liability of $532 based on the standard deduction and exemption credits for a single individual with no dependents.[3] The NPA imposed a late-filing penalty of $135, plus interest.[4]

---

[1] Appellant also received a schedule K-1 from Rockpoint Gas Storage LLC, a California LLC, that reported a loss of $8,623. FTB thus reduced appellant's estimated income by that amount.

[2] FTB applied the standard deduction for a single individual with no dependents. For the 2015 tax year, a single individual under age 65 with no dependents realizing a California gross income of $16,256 or a California adjusted gross income of $13,005 was required to file a California income tax return.

[3] The NPA indicated the amounts assessed would be revised for any differences in filing status, additional deductions, exemptions, or credits when the required tax return was filed. Appellant provided information to indicate a filing status of married filing jointly status and more than two dependents. Residents of some states, including Arizona, may receive a credit (Other State Tax Credit) for taxes paid to the state of residence on income subject to tax in California. However, because appellant never filed a California return for the year at issue, the NPA was not revised.

[4] Since appellant did not challenge the late-filing penalty, other than asserting no tax was due, we are not discussing the penalty.

5. Appellant's federal income tax transcript for 2015 indicated appellant filed a federal return as married filing jointly and that appellant had self-employment income of $99,160.
6. Appellant timely protested the NPA by a letter dated August 2, 2017. Following protest proceedings, FTB issued a Notice of Action dated October 5, 2017, affirming the NPA. Appellant filed this timely appeal.

DISCUSSION

R&TC section 18501 requires every individual subject to the Personal Income Tax Law to make and file a return with the FTB "stating specifically the items of the individual's gross income from all sources and the deductions and credits allowable," in excess of certain filing thresholds. (R&TC, § 18501(a)(1)-(4).) R&TC section 19087(a) provides that if any taxpayer fails to file a return, FTB at any time "may make an estimate of the net income, from any available information, and may propose to assess the amount of tax, interest and penalties due."

California imposes a tax on the entire taxable income of a nonresident, such as appellant, to the extent it is derived from sources within this state. (R&TC, §§ 17041(b), 17951(a).) When the FTB makes a proposed assessment of additional tax based on an estimate of income, the FTB's initial burden is to show why its proposed assessment is reasonable and rational. (*Todd v. McColgan* (1949) 89 Cal.App.2d 509, 514; *Appeal of Myers* (2001-SBE-001) 2019 WL 1187160.) An assessment based on unreported income is presumed correct when the taxing agency introduces a minimal factual foundation to support the assessment. (*In re Olshan* (9th Cir. 2004) 356 F.3d 1078, 1084 [citing *Palmer v. Internal Revenue Service* (9th Cir. 1997) 116 F.3d 1309, 1312]; *Appeal of Bailey* (92-SBE-001) 1992 WL 44503.)

Once the FTB has met its initial burden, the proposed assessment of additional tax is presumed correct and the taxpayer has the burden of proving it to be wrong. (*Todd v. McColgan*, *supra*, 89 Cal.App.2d at p. 514; *Appeal of Myers*, *supra*.) Unsupported assertions are not sufficient to satisfy a taxpayer's burden of proof. (*Appeal of Magidow* (82-SBE-274) 1982 WL 11930.) In the absence of credible, competent, and relevant evidence showing error in the FTB's determination, the determination must be upheld. (*Appeal of Seltzer* (80-SBE-154) 1980 WL 5068.) A taxpayer's failure to produce evidence that is within his control gives rise to a presumption that such evidence is unfavorable to his case. (*Appeal of Cookston* (83-SBE-048) 1983 WL 15431.)

Here, appellant failed to file a 2015 return, even after FTB issued him a Request. As a result, FTB estimated appellant's 2015 income based on information reported on 2015 Forms 1099-MISC that were issued by California LLCs. Appellant does not dispute that he received the income reported on these two Forms 1099-MISC during 2015. FTB's use of Forms 1099-MISC to estimate appellant's taxable income is both reasonable and rational. (See *Giddio v. Commissioner* (1970) 54 T.C. 1530, 1533; *Andrews v. Commissioner*, T.C. Memo. 1998-316.) Moreover, public records from the California Secretary of State provided by FTB show that both LLCs are registered and located in California. FTB established "a minimal predicate" for its determination. (*Andrews v. Commissioner, supra.*) This evidence sufficiently links appellant with income-producing activity in California, and FTB's initial burden has therefore been met. (See *Williams v. Commissioner* (4th Cir. 1993) 999 F.2d 760, 763-766; *Rapp v. Commissioner* (9th Cir. 1985) 774 F.2d 932, 935.)

Appellant contends that he does not have a filing requirement because he was domiciled in, and was a resident of, Arizona during the tax year at issue. Although there is no dispute that Mindbender and Lakeshow were located in California, appellant argues that because he performed all the work in Arizona, his income is not taxable by California.

California Code of Regulations, title 18, section 17951-4

Taxable income of nonresidents "shall be allocated and apportioned under rules and regulations prescribed by the [FTB]." (R&TC, § 17954.) California Code of Regulations, title 18, (Regulation) section 17951-4 provides income sourcing provisions for a nonresident's trade, business, or profession. Under this regulation, the application of the apportionment rules depends upon whether the taxpayer is carrying on a trade or business within the state, without the state, or a combination thereof; the type of entity conducting that business (i.e., sole proprietorship, partnership, or subchapter S corporation); and whether the business is unitary.

1. Appellant Was Carrying on a Business Within and Without California.

As previously mentioned, California imposes a tax on the taxable income of every nonresident, provided that the nonresident meets the filing status threshold requirements of R&TC section 18501(a). (R&TC, § 17041(b)(2).) "Taxable income of a nonresident" is broadly defined as "gross income and deductions derived from sources within this state." (R&TC, § 17041(i)(1)(B).) Income from sources within this state includes "income from a business, trade or profession carried on within this State . . . ." (Cal. Code Regs., tit. 18, § 17951-2.) Indeed, the statutory provisions make no mention that a nonresident must have a physical presence in the state for California to impose a tax.

Here, appellant received income for his services as a self-employed screenwriter from Mindbender and Lakeshow, which are both California LLCs. Appellant was a resident of Arizona where he performed his services as a self-employed screenwriter. He also received $40,000 of gross income from his services as a self-employed screenwriter from California customers. Consequently, appellant's trade or business as a self-employed screenwriter was carried on within and without the state. We find appellant was carrying on a business within and without California.

2. Appellant Was Conducting Business as a Sole Proprietorship.

The term "sole proprietorship" is not defined in Regulation section 17951-4(c), or in the R&TC. A dictionary definition of a "sole proprietorship" is "[a] business in which one person owns all the assets, owes all the liabilities, and operates in his or her personal capacity." (Black's Law Dict. (10th ed. 2014).) For federal and California income tax purposes, a sole proprietorship neither files income tax returns nor pays income tax. Rather, the owner of the sole proprietorship reports all items of income on his or her individual tax return (i.e., on federal Schedule C) and must pay any taxes due.

Here, there is no dispute that appellant, as the owner of a sole proprietorship, was a self-employed screenwriter providing services to companies producing films and television shows. Therefore, based on the evidence before us, we find that appellant conducted his screenwriter business as a sole proprietorship during 2015.

3. Appellant Was Carrying on a Unitary Business.

Regulation section 17951-4 does not define the term "unitary business," but the definition can be inferred from Regulation section 17951-4(b). Regulation section 17951-4(c) applies to a sole proprietorship carrying on a unitary business. Regulation section 17951-4(b) is its counterpart, applying to "a nonresident's business, trade or profession . . . conducted partly within and partly without the state, and the part within the state is so separate and distinct from and unconnected to the part without the state such that the respective business activities are not part of a unitary business, trade or profession . . . ." A unitary business, therefore, can be defined for purposes of Regulation section 17951-4 as a business, trade, or profession conducted both within and without the state, where the part conducted within the state and the part conducted without the state are *not* so separate and distinct from and unconnected to each other to be separate businesses, trades or professions.

The term "unitary business" has been well-established by judicial precedent by creating criteria for determining whether business activities conducted within and without the state were sufficiently interrelated or dependent upon or contributory to one another to be considered a single, or unitary, business. The California Supreme Court has set forth two alternative tests for determining whether a business is "unitary." In *Butler Bros. v. McColgan* (1941) 17 Cal.2d 664, 678, affd. (1942) 315 U.S. 501 (*Butler Bros.*), the court held that the existence of a unitary business may be established by applying the "three unities test." Under this test, unity exists where there is (1) unity of ownership; (2) unity of operation evidenced by central purchasing, management, accounting, etc.; and (3) unity of use in the centralized executive force and general system of operations. (*Ibid.*) Later, in *Edison California Stores, Inc. v. McColgan* (1947) 30 Cal.2d 472, 481 (*Edison California Stores*), the court developed an alternative test called the "contribution or dependency test" and held that a business was unitary if the operation of the business done within this state depended upon or contributed to the operation of the business outside the state. If either the three unities test or the contribution or dependency test is satisfied, the businesses are deemed unitary. (See *A.M. Castle & Co. v. Franchise Tax Bd.* (1995) 36 Cal.App.4th 1794, 1805.)

In addition, Regulation section 25120(b) provides, in pertinent part, that "[i]n general, the activities of the taxpayer will be considered a single business if there is evidence to indicate that the segments under consideration are integrated with, dependent upon or contribute to each other and the operations of the taxpayer as a whole." In short, while these authorities were established in the context of corporations, the essence of what constitutes a unitary business—i.e., sufficiently interrelated and dependent in-state and out-of-state business activities that render it appropriate for the income and losses to be combined and taxed as one unit—is equally applicable to sole proprietorships. (See, e.g., *Appeal of Johnson* (81-SBE-093) 1981 WL 11819 [applying the former version of Regulation section 17951-4(b) to tax income earned by a unitary business conducted through a sole proprietorship].)

Here, appellant wrote a screenplay for each of the LLCs. Appellant rendered these services to the LLCs in his capacity as an owner of a sole proprietorship. He, thus, conducted a one-service business, which only he controlled and managed. There is no indication that would call into question the conclusion that appellant's services were but one interrelated and interdependent business employing and consuming the same resources. Therefore, under *Butler Bros.*, *Edison California Stores*, and Regulation sections 25120(b) and 17951-4, we find that appellant was conducting a unitary business.

Having determined that appellant conducted a sole proprietorship within and without California, we find that appellant falls under the apportionment rules of Regulation section 17951-4(c). This regulation provides that "[t]he amount of such business income derived from sources within [California] shall be determined in accordance with the provisions of the apportionment rules of the Uniform Division of Income for Tax Purposes Act [(UDITPA)], [s]ections 25120 to 25139, inclusive, R&TC, and the regulations thereunder . . . ." (Cal. Code Regs., tit. 18, § 17951-4(c)(2).) Thus, we next address whether any of appellant's income as a self-employed screenwriter for Mindbender and Lakeshow must be apportioned to California.

California's Market-Based Sales Factor Sourcing Provisions

A taxpayer such as appellant who has income from business activity that is taxable both within and without the state must apportion business income according to the UDITPA. (R&TC, § 25121; see also Cal. Code Regs., tit. 18, § 25121.) "Notwithstanding [R&TC] section 38006, for taxable years beginning on or after January 1, 2013, all business income of an apportioning trade or business, other than an apportioning trade or business described in subdivision (b) of [R&TC] section 25128, shall be apportioned to this state by multiplying the business income by the sales factor." (R&TC, § 25128.7.) The sales factor is a fraction, where the numerator is the taxpayer's total sales in California during the tax year and the denominator is the taxpayer's total sales everywhere during the tax year. (R&TC, § 25134; see also Cal. Code Regs., tit. 18, § 25134.)

For purposes of determining what amount is included in the numerator of the sales factor, R&TC section 25136 governs the assignment of receipts from sales other than sales of tangible personal property, such as service revenue.[5] R&TC section 25136(a)(1) provides that "[s]ales

[5] Both contracts with Mindbender and Lakeshow specifically state they are "work-for-hire" or "work made for hire" contracts. In these types of contracts, the person for whom the work was prepared is considered the author

from services are in [California] to the extent the purchaser of the service received the benefit of the services in [California]." Under the statutory grant of authority of R&TC section 25136(b), the FTB promulgated Regulation 25136-2, which provides detailed market-based sales factor sourcing provisions that implement and interpret R&TC section 25136.

Regulation 25136-2(c) states that "[s]ales from services are assigned to [California] to the extent the customer of the taxpayer receives the benefit of the service in [California]." The term, "benefit of a service is received," is defined as "the location where the taxpayer's customer has either directly or indirectly received value from delivery of that service." (Cal. Code Regs., tit. 18, § 25136-2(b)(1).) Regulation section 25136-2(c)(2) provides that, where a corporation or other business entity is the taxpayer's customer, such as in this case, receipt of the benefit of the service shall be determined under the following cascading rules:

> (A) The location of the benefit of the service shall be presumed to be received in this state to the extent the contract between the taxpayer [i.e., appellant] and the taxpayer's customer[s] [i.e., Mindbender and Lakeshow] or the taxpayer's books and records kept in the normal course of business, notwithstanding the billing address of the taxpayer's customer, indicate the benefit of the service is in this state. This presumption may be overcome by the taxpayer or [FTB] by showing, based on a preponderance of the evidence, that the location (or locations) indicated by the contract or the taxpayer's books and records was not the actual location where the benefit of the service was received.
>
> (B) If neither the contract nor the taxpayer's books and records provide the location where the benefit of the service is received, or the presumption in subparagraph (A) is overcome, then the location (or locations) where the benefit is received shall be reasonably approximated.
>
> (C) If the location where the benefit of the service is received cannot be determined under subparagraph (A) or reasonably approximated under subparagraph (B), then the location where the benefit of the service is received shall be presumed to be in this state if the location from which the taxpayer's customer placed the order for the service is in this state.
>
> (D) If the location where the benefit of the service is received cannot be determined pursuant to subparagraphs (A), (B), or (C), then the benefit of the service shall be in this state if the taxpayer's customer's billing address is in this state.

Here, we are unable to apply the first cascading rule under subparagraph (A). The contract does not specify the location where Mindbender or Lakeshow received the benefit, and, for purposes

of the work "and, unless the parties have expressly agreed otherwise in a written instrument signed by them, owns all of the rights comprised in the copyright." (17 U.S.C. § 201(b).) Therefore, appellant was engaged in a sale of his writing services and not a sale of intangible property (i.e., intellectual property).

of subparagraph (A), Mindbender's and Lakeshow's billing address is irrelevant. Under subparagraph (B), we can reasonably approximate the location where the LLCs received the benefit of appellant's services. "Reasonably approximated" means, in relevant part, "considering all sources of information other than the terms of the contract and the taxpayer's books and records kept in the normal course of business, the location of the market for the benefit of the services . . . is determined in a manner that is consistent with the activities of [the LLCs] to the extent such information is available to [appellant]." (Cal. Code Regs., tit. 18, § 25136-2(b)(7).)

Public records from the California Secretary of State provided by FTB show that both Mindbender and Lakeshow are registered and located in California. Moreover, appellant's contracts with Mindbender and Lakeshow both list California addresses. Appellant also concedes that Mindbender and Lakeshow are California LLCs. Based on the evidence in the appeal record, we find that it was both reasonable and rational for FTB to conclude that both LLCs received the benefit of appellant's services within California. Because we have determined that the LLCs received the benefit of appellant's services in California under Regulation section 25136-2(b)(2)(B), there is no need to discuss the remaining cascading rules.

In sum, pursuant to the provisions of the UDITPA relating to the sale of services and the regulations thereunder, appellant's physical presence does not determine whether he had income derived from California, but rather it is determined by where the benefits of appellant's services were received. Having established that income from Mindbender and the income from Lakeshow are sourced to California, FTB estimated appellant's income as $31,377, based upon income appellant received from Mindbender and Lakeshow. Therefore, we find that FTB met its initial burden of showing that the proposed assessment for the 2015 tax year is reasonable and rational and that appellant did not meet his burden of proving that the proposed assessment, which is presumed correct, is erroneous.

HOLDING

Appellant received taxable income from a California source in 2015.

DISPOSITION

FTB's proposed assessment is sustained.

DocuSigned by:
Patrick J. Kusiak
8F20779E0CD743F...
Patrick J. Kusiak
Administrative Law Judge

We concur:

DocuSigned by:
Jeffrey Margolis
5E9822FBB1BA41B...
Jeffrey I. Margolis
Administrative Law Judge

DocuSigned by:
Nguyen Dang
4D465973EB44469...
Nguyen Dang
Administrative Law Judge

Exhibit "F"

Filed 6/29/20

CERTIFIED FOR PUBLICATION

IN THE COURT OF APPEAL OF THE STATE OF CALIFORNIA

FIRST APPELLATE DISTRICT

DIVISION THREE

ALAN STEUER, as Trustee, etc., et al., Plaintiffs and Respondents, v. FRANCHISE TAX BOARD, Defendant and Appellant.	A154691 (City & County of San Francisco Super. Ct. No. CGC-16-556126)

Franchise Tax Board (FTB) appeals from a summary judgment order holding (1) a trust's income, even if entirely derived from California sources, is only taxable under residence-based taxation; and (2) the sole beneficiary of the Paula Trust was a contingent beneficiary. The law is well settled that individuals regardless of their residences are taxed on all income derived from California sources. (Rev. & Tax. Code, § 17041, subd. (i)(1)(B).)[1] The trial court found the Revenue and Taxation Code, however, only imposes taxes on trust income that can be apportioned according to the number of resident fiduciaries, rather than taxing all California source income. (§ 17743.) Thus, Paula Trust was only required to pay tax on one-half of its

[1] Undesignated statutory references are to the Revenue and Taxation Code.

total California-source income, because out of its two trustees, only one was a California resident.

We reverse, in part, and affirm, in part. Based on our reading of the statute's provisions as a whole, we conclude the Revenue and Taxation Code imposes taxes on the entire amount of trust income derived from California sources, regardless of the residency of the trust's fiduciaries. However, we affirm the trial court's ruling finding the sole beneficiary's interest in the trust income was contingent.

BACKGROUND

Raymond J. Syufy established the Paula Trust for the sole benefit of his daughter Paula Syufy Medeiros (Medeiros), a California resident. The Paula Trust has two cotrustees—a California resident and a Maryland resident, the fiduciaries.

Paula Trust held a limited partnership interest in Syufy Enterprises LP, which in 2007 sold stock to Century Theatres, Inc.; Century Theatre Holdings, LLC; Cinemark USA, Inc.; and Cinemark Holdings, Inc. Some of the capital gain income from the stock sale was allocated to Paula Trust. Paula Trust's 2007 tax return reported gross income in the amount of $2,965,099—$2,831,336 of capital gain including the stock sale—and the trust paid California income tax in the amount of $223,425.

In 2012, however, the trustees filed an amended 2007 California fiduciary income tax return, requesting a refund of $150,655 in allegedly overpaid income taxes. At the time, Paula Trust claimed the capital gain was incorrectly reported as California-source income. The trustees declared they were "required to apportion the stock gain as California source and non-California-source income . . . according to the number of trustees resident in California" based on section 17743. (All caps omitted.) Section 17743 provides: "Where the taxability of income under this chapter depends on the residence of the fiduciary and there are two or more fiduciaries for the trust, the income taxable . . . shall be apportioned according to the number of fiduciaries resident in this state . . . ." (§ 17743.) According to the trustees, only one-half of the capital gain apportioned to the California trustee was taxable income, while the other half, apportioned to the Maryland trustee, was not taxable. After an administrative appeal, the Board of Equalization rejected the requested refund, and Paula Trust filed a tax refund suit in 2016.

The trial court granted Paula Trust's motion for summary judgment, and summary adjudication in the alternative, holding both that Medeiros is a contingent beneficiary and that "Paula Trust's California taxable income is determined by apportioning its income pursuant to Rev. & Tax. Code § 17743"—one-half to its California trustee and one-half to its Maryland trustee. The trial court then entered judgment ordering a refund in the amount of $150,655 of tax, plus interest of $68,955.70.

DISCUSSION[2]

We review the trial court's ruling on the summary judgment motion and statutory construction de novo. (*Regents of University of California v. Superior Court* (1999) 20 Cal.4th 509, 531.) Applying a taxing statute to uncontradicted facts is a question of law, and we are not bound to accept the

---

[2] During briefing in this case, FTB filed a request for judicial notice of an additional court record. We deferred ruling on the request until the merits of the appeal. (See *People v. Preslie* (1977) 70 Cal.App.3d 486, 493–494.) We now exercise our discretion and deny the request. Appellate courts are not required to take judicial notice of documents that were not presented to the trial court. (*McMahan v. City and County of San Francisco* (2005) 127 Cal.App.4th 1368, 1373, fn. 2.)

trial court's findings of fact. (*Communications Satellite Corp. v. Franchise Tax Bd.* (1984) 156 Cal.App.3d 726, 746.)

I. TAXABLE INCOME OF TRUSTS

Paula Trust contends that under a plain reading of section 17743, the taxable amount of the trust's income depends on the number of trust fiduciaries who are residents of California, regardless of whether the income is derived from California sources. The trial court agreed, determining "Rev. & Tax. Code § 17041(i) and Rev. & Tax. Code § 17951 *et seq.*, which collectively define taxable income of nonresidents"—and requires taxing all California-source income—"do not apply to trusts because those statutes apply only to nonresidents." The court ruled "in light of the differences between trust [*sic*] and individual taxpayers, it is not absurd or unreasonable that the Legislature enacted different tax schemes for each."

We are not persuaded by this interpretation of the statute. Construing a statute requires starting with the statutory language, giving words their ordinary meaning, and applying the language if it is clear and unambiguous. (*Goldman v. Franchise Tax Bd.* (2012) 202 Cal.App.4th 1193, 1199.) We resort to extrinsic sources, such as legislative history, the statute's purpose, and public policy, to determine legislative intent if the language is ambiguous on its face or permits more than one reasonable interpretation. (*Ibid.*) After engaging in that review here, we arrive at the opposite conclusion.

A. Basis of Taxable Income

Section 17041 articulates two bases for imposing personal income tax in California. First, residents are generally taxed on all of their income, regardless of its source. (§ 17041, subd. (a)(1) ["There shall be imposed for each taxable year upon the entire taxable income of every resident of this state"].) This provision "ensure[s] that individuals who are present in the state, and receiving the benefits and protections of its laws, contribute to it by paying taxes on all income regardless of its source." (*Paine v. Franchise Tax Bd.* (2004) 118 Cal.App.4th 63, 67.)

Second, nonresident taxpayers are taxed on "gross income . . . derived from sources within this state"—California-source income. (§ 17041, subd. (i)(1)(B); see § 17951, subd. (a) ["For purposes of computing 'taxable income of a nonresident or part-year resident' under . . . Section 17041, in the case of nonresident taxpayers the gross income includes only the gross income from sources within this state"].)

Paula Trust contends the definition of "resident"—a term it argues is defined only as "individuals" or "natural persons"—definitively establishes these tax rules on California-source income do not apply to trusts which are simply abstractions. (§§ 17005, 17014, 17015.) However, the statutory definition for "resident" states that it "*includes*" individuals who are in or domiciled in this state. (§ 17014, italics added.) It does not expressly limit the definition of "resident" to "individuals" or "natural persons." (*Ibid.*)

More importantly, Paula Trust's narrow reading of the term "resident" fails to assess that term in context. When harmonized with the additional provisions and statutory framework of the Revenue and Taxation Code, the statute establishes that trusts are taxed on the same basis as individuals. (See § 17002 [statutory definitions govern "[e]xcept where the *context otherwise requires*" (italics added)]; see also *Lungren v. Deukmejian* (1988) 45 Cal.3d 727, 735 ["the 'plain meaning' rule does not prohibit a court from determining whether the literal meaning of a statute comports with its purpose or whether such a construction of one provision is consistent with other provisions of the statute"].)

Revenue and Taxation Code section 17731 incorporates the federal Internal Revenue Code trust provisions, which compute a trust's taxable income "*in the same manner as in the case of an individual* . . . . The tax shall be computed on such taxable income and shall be paid by the fiduciary." (26 U.S.C. § 641(b), italics added; see Rev. & Tax. Code, § 17731 subd. (a) ["Subchapter J of Chapter 1 of Subtitle A of the Internal Revenue Code, relating to estates, trusts, beneficiaries, and decedents, shall apply, except as otherwise provided"].) Revenue and Taxation Code section 17041, subdivision (e) similarly mandates calculating a trust's taxable income as if the trust were an individual. (See Rev. & Tax. Code, § 17041, subd. (e) ["There shall be imposed for each taxable year upon the taxable income of every . . . trust . . . taxes equal to the amount computed under subdivision (a) for an individual having the same amount of taxable income"].) Read together, Revenue and Taxation Code section 17041, subdivision (i) directs the taxable income of any nonresident to include income from a California source, and trusts compute taxable income in the same manner as individuals. As a result, trusts are taxed on all California-source income without regard to the residence of fiduciaries.

Even if we were to accept Paula Trust's argument that section 17041, subdivision (e) simply sets equal tax rates for trusts and individuals rather than requires taxing a trust's California-source income, the provision nonetheless requires treating individuals and trusts similarly under the Revenue and Taxation Code. (See *Robinson v. Franchise Tax Board* (1981) 120 Cal.App.3d 72, 77, fn. 4 ["California generally taxes the income of a trust as if it were an individual (§ 17731) under the Personal Income Tax Law"].)

B. Apportionment of Trust Income

The plain language of section 17743 and its rules require taxing all of a trust's California-source income and then apportioning only income derived outside of California according to the number of resident fiduciaries. (§ 17743; Cal. Code Regs., tit. 18, § 17743.) They do not, as Paula Trust argues, exclude trusts from the provisions taxing all California-source income or make the amount of a trust's income taxable dependent solely on the number and residence of trust fiduciaries.

The income of a trust is taxable to the estate or trust. (§ 17742, subd. (a).) Section 17742 provides, in relevant part, the "tax applies . . . to the entire taxable income of a trust, *if* the fiduciary or [noncontingent] beneficiary . . . is a resident." (§ 17742, subd. (a), italics added; see *McCulloch v. Franchise Tax Bd.* (1964) 61 Cal.2d 186, 195 [tax is appropriate "since that state provides to the trustees the protection requisite to the receipt and control of the disposition of trust income"].) This provision assumes only one resident fiduciary or beneficiary. Recognizing that trusts may have multiple fiduciaries who live outside of California, section 17743—as its title "Trust; Taxability dependent on residence of fiduciary" indicates—addresses the taxation of income received by a trust with multiple trustees with different residences. (§§ 17743, 17744.)

Section 17743 then applies in the limited circumstance "[w]here the taxability of income under this chapter *depends on the residence* of the fiduciary"—meaning the income is derived from non-California sources since the only basis for taxing the income is residency—"and there are two or more fiduciaries for the trust . . . ." (§ 17743, italics added.) In that situation, the non-California-source income that is taxable under section 17742 "shall be apportioned according to the number of fiduciaries resident in this state . . . ." (§ 17743.)

Even if we stop reviewing section 17743's language there, the statute demonstrates that only non-California-source income must be apportioned to resident fiduciaries. (§ 17743.) The statute, however, goes further, noting that apportionment must be "pursuant to rules and regulations prescribed by the Franchise Tax Board"—rules that are expressly incorporated into the statute and language which Paula Trust curiously ignores.

The FTB regulations provide: "[T]he trust is taxable upon (a) all net income . . . from business carried on within this State, from real or tangible personal property located in this State, and from intangible personal property having a business or taxable situs in this State . . . and; (b) that proportion of the net income . . . from all other sources which the number of fiduciaries who are residents of this State bears to the total number of fiduciaries." (Cal. Code Regs., tit. 18, § 17743, 1st par. (Regulation 17743).) The statute is clear. The FTB promulgated rules for apportioning trust income when there are multiple resident and nonresident fiduciaries. The statute requires taxpayers to follow those rules. When we read the statute and the regulation together, as required by the plain language of the statute, a trust is taxed on all California-source income, regardless of whether the fiduciary is a nonresident or not. Then, non-California-source income is apportioned between California and non-California fiduciaries. (Cal. Code Regs., tit. 18, § 17743; see §§ 17041, subds. (e), (i)(1)(B), 17731, subd. (a), 17743.)

We reject Paula Trust's circular argument this regulation is invalid or fails to comport with the plain terms of the statute. (See Gov. Code, § 11342.2 [regulations promulgated by state agencies must be "consistent and not in conflict with the statute and reasonably necessary to effectuate the purpose of the statute"].) As noted above, the regulation properly follows the statute and provides rules for apportioning only non-California-source income to resident fiduciaries as required by section 17743.

C. Legislative History

"Although we need not go further because the statutory language is unambiguous, we will 'look to legislative history to confirm our plain-meaning construction of [the] statutory language.'" (*Becerra v. Superior Court* (2020) 44 Cal.App.5th 897, 920, citing *Hughes v. Pair* (2009) 46 Cal.4th 1035, 1046.)

1. 1935 and 1937 Personal Income Tax Acts

The Personal Income Tax Act of 1935 (1935 Code), modeled after the federal tax structure, treats a trust as a separate economic entity. (*McCulloch v. Franchise Tax Bd.*, *supra*, 61 Cal.2d at p. 191.) The 1935 Code imposed taxes upon "the entire net income of every resident of this State and upon the net income of every nonresident which is derived from sources within this State . . . ." (Stats. 1935, ch. 329, § 5(a), p. 1093.) Additionally, it created the rule that the "taxes imposed by this act upon individuals shall apply to, and be imposed upon, the income of . . . property held in trust" and requires computing the trust's tax "upon the net income of the estate or trust . . . except" as otherwise provided. (Stats. 1935, ch. 329, § 12(a), (b), pp. 1103–1104; see § 17731.) These provisions parallel those in the Internal Revenue Code, taxing foreign trusts on the amounts of "[g]ross income from sources within the United States . . . ." (26 U.S.C. § 643(a)(6)(B).)

Section 12(b) of the 1935 Code created a series of provisions applicable to trusts. (Stats. 1935, ch. 329, § 12(b), pp. 1104–1105.) Among them were rules identifying the taxable income of a trust as "(1) The income from real property and tangible personal property located and from business transacted in this State. [¶] (2) The income from intangible property with a situs in this State. [¶] (3) The income from real property and tangible personal property located outside this State and the income from intangible property with a situs outside this State" when one of the various combinations of residences of beneficiaries, fiduciaries, or settlors identified in an exhaustive list was present.[3] (Stats. 1935, ch. 329, § 12(b), p. 1104.)

Section 12 of the 1935 Code also created language essentially similar to current Revenue and Taxation Code section 17743: "Where the taxability of income under this section depends on the residence of the fiduciary and there are two or more fiduciaries for the estate or trust, the income taxable under this section shall be apportioned according to the number of fiduciaries resident in this State, such apportionment being determined according to rules and regulations prescribed by the commissioner." (Stats. 1935, ch. 329, § 12(b), p. 1104.)

The parties primarily dispute the significance of the 1937 Personal Income Tax Act amendments (1937 amendments), which largely eliminated section 12(b), including subsections (1) and (2)—the rules for identifying taxable California-source income of trusts. (See Stats. 1937, ch. 668, § 8, p.

---

[3] Those combinations are: "(A) Where the beneficiary and the fiduciary and the settlor are all residents of this State. [¶] (B) Where the beneficiary and the fiduciary are residents of this State regardless of the residence of the settlor. [¶] (C) Where the beneficiary and the settlor are residents of this State regardless of the residence of the fiduciary. [¶] (D) Where the beneficiary is a resident of this State regardless of the residence of the fiduciary and the settlor. [¶] (E) Where the fiduciary is a resident of this State regardless of the residence of the beneficiary and the settlor. [¶] (F) Where the settlor is a resident of this State regardless of the residence of the beneficiary and the fiduciary. [¶] (G) Where the fiduciary and the settlor are residents of this State regardless of the residence of the beneficiary." (Stats. 1935, ch. 329, § 12(b)(3), p. 1104.)

1844.) Paula Trust contends this demonstrates the Legislature's intent to entirely eliminate taxing trusts on income derived from California sources. We disagree.

The 1937 amendments did not alter the substantive provisions, first, requiring taxing individuals on California-source income and, second, requiring the "net income of the estate or trust shall be computed in the same manner and on the same basis as the case of an individual." (See Stats. 1937, ch. 668 [not amending § 5], § 8, pp. 1844–1846 [amending § 12(c), (d) computing income].) The Legislature retained section 12(c)'s language apportioning taxable income to instances "[w]here the taxability . . . depends on the residence"—tax income derived outside California when it could only be reached by virtue of the fiduciaries' residence. (See Stats. 1937, ch. 668, § 8, pp. 1844–1845 [amending § 12(c), (d) computing income].)

If the Legislature eliminated California's ability to tax a trust's California-source income, the phrase in current Revenue and Taxation Code section 17743 "[w]here the taxability . . . depends on the residence" would serve no purpose. (See *People v. Hudson* (2006) 38 Cal. 4th 1002, 1010 [interpretations that render statutory terms meaningless as surplusage should be avoided].) Residency would be the only basis for taxing trust income, so there would be no reason to identify circumstances under which taxation depends on residence. However, because taxability of income depends on two distinct bases—residence or California-source income—this legislative history and the language that the 1937 amendments retained in section 12 of the 1935 Code demonstrate that the Legislature intended trusts would continue to be taxed on California-source income. (*Davis v. Franchise Tax Board* (1977) 71 Cal.App.3d 998, 1002.)

Relying on *Gikas v. Zolin* (1993) 6 Cal.4th 841, Paula Trust nonetheless argues the Legislature intended to eliminate tax on trust income from " 'sources within this state' " because that language is present in sections 17734 and 17953—relating to determining the source of income and taxability of a nonresident *beneficiary's* income based on source—and absent from sections 17742 and 17743—determining taxability of a *trust's* income based on residency. (See *id.* at pp. 851–852 [determining only acquittals in criminal proceedings have a preclusive effect on subsequent administrative proceedings]; §§ 17734, 17953.) This reliance is misplaced.

The *Gikas* court noted the omission of language from one specific section of a statute demonstrated the Legislature's intent to limit the reach of that *specific* section. Here, in contrast, Paula Trust argues the omission of California-source language from two sections of a statute—sections 17734 and 17953—indicates the intention to eliminate it from another—sections 17743 and 17744. (§§ 17734, 17743, 17744, 17953.) *Gikas* does not support that interpretation.

2. Administrative Interpretations

The contemporaneous comments to regulations interpreting these trust provisions bolster our holding. (See *Western Oil & Gas Assn. v. Air Resources Board* (1984) 37 Cal.3d 502, 520 [as a "contemporaneous construction of a statute by an administrative agency charged with its enforcement, the [agency's] view is entitled to great weight"].) Regulation 17743 was originally promulgated in 1936 after the Legislature passed the 1935 Code. The 1936 regulation contained the bifurcated, two-step apportionment method that appears in current regulation governing apportionment. (Cal. Code Regs., tit. 18, § 17743; cf. Cal. Franchise Tax Bd., Legal Ruling No. 238 (Oct. 27, 1959) ["When the entire income of a trust is derived from sources outside of

California, and at least one of the trustees and at least one of the beneficiaries are California residents, both Sections 17743 and 17744 of the Personal Income Tax Law are applicable. Each section is applied after deducting from total income that portion attributable to the other section"].)

After the 1937 amendments, the Franchise Tax Commissioner acknowledged new regulations were "necessitated by the amendments to the act . . . ." However, the revised 1938 regulations left the rules for apportioning trust income substantively the same. In the preface to the revised 1938 regulations, the commissioner characterized the 1937 amendments to these Revenue and Taxation Code trust provisions as "minor." Indeed, the 1937 amendments also eliminated section 12(b)(3) which previously identified trust income as including non-California-source income and its listed beneficiary and fiduciary combinations for determining when this income could be taxed. (See Stats. 1937, ch. 668, § 8, pp. 1838–1839.) Rather than eliminating the ability to tax trusts based on their California-source income, it appears, as relevant here, the amendments primarily removed superfluous language.

D. Effectuating Legislative Intent

Our reading and interpretation of these tax statutes effectuates the purpose of the statute and avoids results that are contrary to legislative intent. (See *Taiheiyo Cement U.S.A., Inc. v. Franchise Tax Bd.* (2012) 204 Cal.App.4th 254, 259–260; *Microsoft Corp. v. Franchise Tax Bd.* (2006) 39 Cal.4th 750, 759 [preferring an interpretation in favor of a taxpayer only when a tax statute's language is ambiguous].) Our Supreme Court has noted although " 'the complexity of the trust itself and of the relations of the parties thereto complicates the problem of effective taxation, it should not obstruct the claims of a state to tax trust income, so far as possible, as it would in the absence of a trust. . . . It should, therefore, be taxed so far as possible upon the same basis as other taxpayers.' " (*McCulloch v. Franchise Tax Board*, *supra*, 61 Cal.2d at p. 197, fn. 9.) The trial court's decision upends this policy.

Paula Trust readily admits the trial court's ruling results in California's being unable to tax trust income if the trust does not have any resident trustees or noncontingent beneficiaries. However, it asserts this interpretation does not result in the trust's avoiding taxes on California-source income. Instead, Paula Trust argues the portion of the income that is not taxed to the trust will be taxed under either section 17734 or section 17953 if distributions are made to nonresident beneficiaries, or section 17745 if a distribution is made to a resident beneficiary.

This is unconvincing. First, trusts and individuals are taxed on their income in the year in which it is received. (§§ 17041, subds. (a), (e); *McCulloch v. Franchise Tax Board*, *supra*, 61 Cal.2d at pp. 189–190 [trusts incurred tax liability on its income earned "during *each of the five prior years as it was earned*"].) The trial court's ruling effectively eliminates this rule since a trust without resident trustees or beneficiaries will not be taxed on any annual accumulated income.

Second, section 17745 is only applicable "[i]f the trustee fails to pay the tax for the trust *annually as it earns the income* . . . ." (*McCulloch v. Franchise Tax Board*, *supra*, 61 Cal.2d at pp. 191, 192 & fn. 4 [interpreting former § 18106, now current § 17745]; see § 17745, subd. (b) ["If no taxes have been paid on the current or accumulated income of the trust because the resident beneficiary's interest in the trust was contingent such income shall be taxable to the beneficiary when distributed or distributable to him or her"].) Rather than excusing a trust from making tax payments on its annual income, section 17745 is a mechanism to recover income if the trust fails to pay the appropriate amount of taxes.

Third, there is no requirement that the trust distribute all income to the beneficiary. And a beneficiary is only taxed on the amount of trust income that is distributed, not the total amount accumulated by the trust in a particular year. (§§ 17041, subd. (a), 17734.) Thus, the beneficiary may be subject to a different tax rate in the year of distribution than the trust would have been in the year the California-source income was received. (§§ 17041, subds. (a)(1) [identifying higher tax rates for larger amounts of annual income received], (e).)

Accordingly, we conclude Paula Trust has not shown section 17743 eliminates taxation on a trust's California-source income. The trial court erred in granting Paula Trust's motion for summary judgment on that issue.

II. CONTINGENT BENEFICIARY

Finally, FTB contends the trial court erred finding that Medeiros is a contingent beneficiary as a matter of law. We do not agree.

Under section 17742, trust income may also be taxed based on residency, without regard to source, if there is a noncontingent California beneficiary. (§ 17742.) Where a trustee has absolute discretion to allocate net trust income to the beneficiary, the beneficiary has a contingent interest in the distribution. (*Estate of Canfield* (1947) 80 Cal.App.2d 443, 451–452; Cal. Franchise Tax Bd., Technical Advice Mem. 2006-0002 (Feb. 17, 2006) p. 2 ["A resident beneficiary whose interest in a trust is subject to the sole and absolute discretion of the trustee holds a contingent interest in the trust"].) "The intention of the settlor as shown by the document creating the trust is the most important single element in the determination of the rights of the trustee." (*Estate of Miller* (1964) 230 Cal.App.2d 888, 908–909 (*In re Miller*).)

Accordingly, we review the trust document to determine whether there are any limitations on a trustee's discretion to distribute income to a beneficiary. (See Cal. Franchise Tax Bd., Technical Advice Mem. 2006-0002 (Feb. 17, 2006) pp. 3–4 ["[t]he extent of the interest of the beneficiary of a trust depends upon the manifestation of intention of the settlor"].)

Here, the Paula Trust document grants "sole absolute discretion" to the cotrustees to make distributions of trust income and principal, but that authority "shall not *require* the Trustee to make any distribution to any person." (Italics added.) Instead, the document simply authorized, rather than mandated, the trustees to distribute as much net income or principal of the trust as the trustee deemed to be in the beneficiary's best interests, but the determination of the amount to distribute was also in the trustee's sole absolute discretion.

This "best interests" language does not, as FTB asserts and relying on *In re Miller*, limit the trustee's discretion. In that case, the settlor intended the trust to support one of the beneficiaries, and the trustee owed a duty "to make allowances for [the beneficiary's] support and maintenance . . . ." (*In re Miller*, *supra*, 230 Cal.App.2d at p. 909.) The court determined the trustee abused his discretion by failing to make any distributions "sufficient to keep [the beneficiary] alive, let alone to maintain her in the condition and situation to which she was accustomed." (*Id*. at pp. 909–910.)

The trust's provisions here are quite distinguishable. The trustees are not *required* to make distributions to support Medeiros. Although the trust included various examples of distributions that would be in the best interest of the beneficiary—including permitting the beneficiary to travel for education or pleasure, purchasing a residence or investing in business—the trust expressly stated these examples were "intended solely as a precatory guide to the Trustee and shall in no way be construed to alter, limit or enlarge the discretions and powers conferred upon the Trustee by any other provision hereof nor to require the Trustee to make any distribution to any beneficiary." If anything, the decision in *In re Miller* is only relevant here for the limited and uncontroversial premise that "[e]ven where the trustee has discretion . . . , the court will not permit him to abuse the discretion." (*In re Miller, supra*, 230 Cal.App.2d at p. 907.) Like the trial court, we find the trust instrument's plain and unambiguous terms provided the trustees with sole and absolute discretion to make distributions to Medeiros.

FTB further asserts aside from reviewing the trust instrument, there must be a factual inquiry to determine the specific nature of a beneficiary. In FTB's opinion, the facts demonstrate Medeiros's interest in the trust income is noncontingent since the trustees notified her of future distributions, she relied on those distributions in making certain financial choices, and she directed how the trustees would pay the distributions.[4]

Those actions do not change that the distributions are conditioned upon the trustee's discretion to approve or make them. (See *NC Dept of Rev v. Kim Rice Kaestner 1992 Trust* (2019) 588 U.S. ___ , ___ [139 S.Ct. 2213, 2223] ["by reserving sole discretion to the trustee, the Trust agreement still deprived

---

[4] The unique circumstances presented in *Flato v. Commissioner of Internal Revenue* (5th Cir. 1952) 195 F.2d 580—a trust in which two brothers were both trustees and beneficiaries for themselves, and a third brother beneficiary—do not help FTB's argument. (*Id.* at p. 581.) The beneficiaries in that case requested and received whatever amounts of trust income they desired, and the Fifth Circuit determined the trial court properly reviewed the " 'whole nexus of relations between the settlor, the trustee and the beneficiary' . . . ." (*Id.* at pp. 582–583.) However, the court limited the ruling to that particular case, noting "the beneficiaries possessed such command over the distribution of the income of the trusts, such income, whether distributed or not, is taxable to them." (*Id.* at p. 583 & fn. 3.)

[beneficiaries] of any entitlement to demand distributions or to direct the use of the Trust assets in their favor"].) As FTB's own technical memorandum notes, a contingent beneficiary "cannot compel the trustee to give him any portion of the income where the trust gives the trustee absolute discretion as to the amounts of income to distribute." (Cal. Franchise Tax Bd., Technical Advice Mem. 2006-0002 (Feb. 17, 2006) p. 3, fn. 3.) While Medeiros could certainly request distributions or assign distributions once she received them to other trusts or various financial arrangements, she "cannot be certain that [s]he will ever enjoy any of [the] proceeds of the trust. Consequently, where the extent of the interest of the beneficiary is dependent upon the exercise of discretion by the trustee, that interest is contingent." (*Ibid.*)

The settlor intended the trustees to have absolute discretion, and we affirm the trial court's finding Medeiros is a contingent beneficiary.

DISPOSITION

The summary judgment in favor of Paula Trust is reversed. On remand the trial court shall enter an order of summary adjudication of Medeiros being a contingent beneficiary.

Jackson, J.

WE CONCUR:

Fujisaki, Acting P. J.

Petrou, J.

A154691/*Steuer v. Franchise Tax Bd.*

A154691/Steuer v. Franchise Tax Bd.

Trial Court:	Superior Court of the City and County of San Francisco
Trial Judge:	Harold E. Kahn, J.
Counsel:	Xavier Becerra, Attorney General, Diane Spencer Shaw, Assistant Attorney General, Lucy F. Wang, Karen W. Yiu, and Heather B. Hoesterey, Deputy Attorneys General, for Defendant and Appellant.
	Antolin Agarwal, Edwin P. Antolin, Monty Agarwal, and Rachel L. Chanin for Plaintiffs and Respondents.

Cooley

Exhibit "G"

Section 1202 Qualified Small Business Stock Cheat Sheet

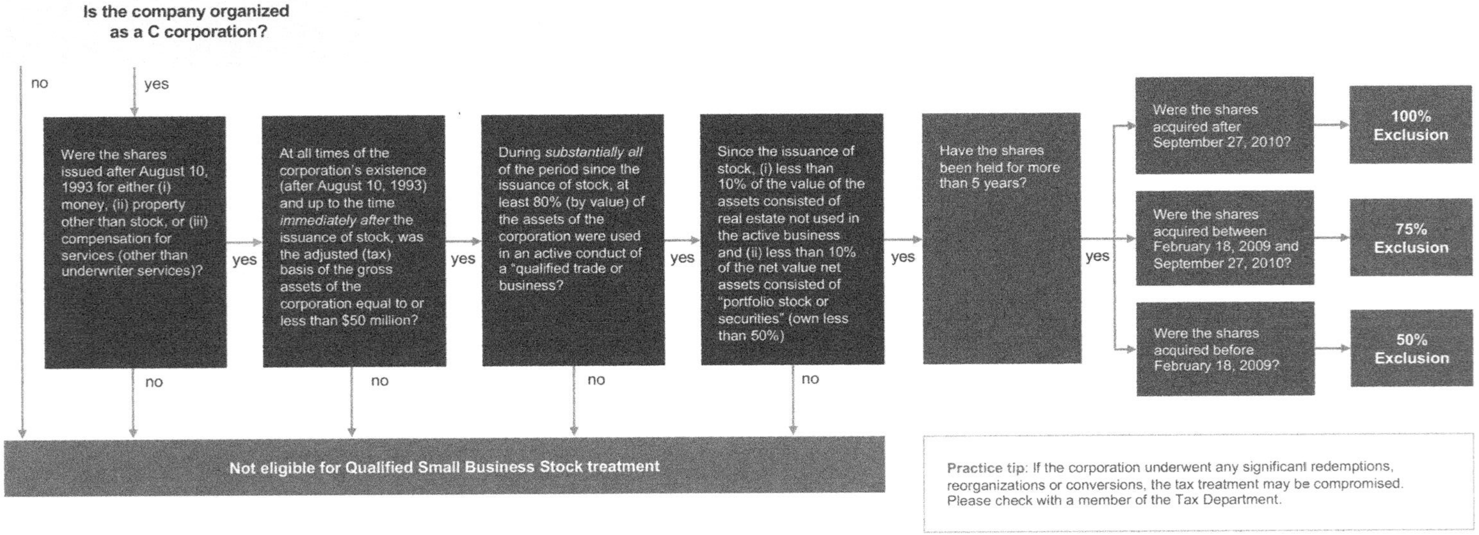

This document is intended for internal use to provide the general rules regarding Qualified Small Business Stock. Each company has its own specific facts that require separate analysis and this document does not constitute the written advice of the Tax Department. We strongly advise discussing each specific case with a member of the Tax Department.

Cooley

Section 1202 Qualified Small Business Stock Cheat Sheet

- The entity must be a C corporation. 1202(c)(1). Special entities like REITs, RICs, REMICs, DISCs, cooperatives and other pass through entities (S corporations) are not eligible. 1202(e)(4).

- The corporation MUST be under the $50 million threshold at all times after August 10, 1993 and through the time of the share issuance. 1202(d)(1)(A).
- Note that the test says immediately after the share issuance. That means that it includes the issuance (and thus counts any money or property contributed as part of the issuance) in calculating the limitation. 1202(d)(1)(B).
- The adjusted (tax) basis of the aggregate gross assets includes the fair market value of any assets contributed to the corporation (rather than the adjusted tax basis) determined as of the date the assets were contributed. 1202(d)(2)(B).

A "qualified trade or business" means a business ***other*** than:

- performance of services in the fields of:
  - health
  - law
  - engineering
  - architecture
  - accounting
  - actuarial science
  - performing arts
  - consulting
  - athletics
  - financial services
  - brokerage services
  - or any trade or business where the principal asset is the reputation or the skill or one or more of its employees
- Banking, Financing, Insurance, Leasing, Investing or similar business.
- Farming, Gardening, Growing or other Agricultural Business.
- Mining, Drilling or other Extraction type Business.
- Operation of a Hotel, Motel, Restaurant or other Hospitality Services. 1202(e)(3).

- For purposes of the active business test, a parent corporation "looks through" to its subsidiaries and counts a "ratable" share of the subsidiaries' business assets and business activities for purposes of the test. 1202(e)(5)(A).
- A parent must own more than 50% of the combined voting power of all classes of stock entitled to vote or more than 50 percent of the value of all outstanding stock. 1202(e)(5)(C). Any ownership of less than 50% constitutes a portfolio investment that is not considered active. 1202(e)(5)(B).
- A reasonable amount of working capital can be counted as part of the business assets of a corporation. 1202(e)(6)(A).
- This may include investments that are reasonably expected to be used within 2 years to fund research and experimentation expenses of a qualified business. However, a corporation in existence more than 2 years is limited to 50% of its assets under this exception. 1202(e)(6)(B).

- If stock qualifies, then some or all of the gain from the sale may be excluded by the selling shareholder based on when the shareholder acquired the shares
- Remember that the rules regarding capital gains treatment have changed – thus, calculating the exclusion under the 50% and 75% exclusions requires more complicated calculations (also AMT and the 3.8% Medicare tax need to be considered in certain instances).
- A shareholder has a limitation on the amount of stock that is excluded under Section 1202 equal to the greater of:
  - $10 million (reduced by any amount excluded in prior years from sales of the same corporation stock); and
  - 10 times the taxpayer's aggregate adjusted bases of qualified small business stock issued by the corporation.
  - Section 1202(b)(1).

Made in the USA
Monee, IL
04 November 2026

67378658R00066